"The First Time...Because Everything Has a Beginning"

"A love letter to every young girl who didn't know that she had a voice"

Carolyn Harris-Hutchinson

The First Time…because everything has a beginning
Copyright © 2020 by Carolyn Harris-Hutchinson

All rights reserved. No part of this book may be reproduced or transmitted in any form or by any means without written permission from the author.

Printed in USA

Writers Concierge Publishing Services
Contact: bevjonesdurr@writersconcierge.com

Acknowledgements

One Sunday, while visiting what had once been my home church, somewhere during worship I heard a voice which said "It's time." Immediately, I knew exactly what was being conveyed with those two words "It's time." I wasn't confused, nor did I search to see where the voice was coming from. I instinctively knew and dare say that I probably had anticipated this moment (unconsciously) for quite some time. With the declaration of those two words, I knew and acknowledged that it was indeed time to birth this book. But just like in any other "birth" experience, there are always at least one and in most instances, many people who contributed to bringing the "new life" into fruition.

I give thanks for the women who comprised the writing group where the beginning of this writing process began. For your listening ears, encouraging comments, and non-judgmental spirits, I give thanks. For impromptu conversations that seemed to occur each time I mentioned that I was "writing a book." For those who quietly whispered "it happened to me too." To my parents who created me, to those who mentored me, those who challenged me and those who simply loved me unconditionally. To those who took the time, shared their smiles and let me know that it would be alright. To each and every one of you because you are a part of whom I am today. I give thanks.

Dedication

I dedicate this book to my children (Charles, Malcolm and Nia). You three represent the best of me and I love you more than you can ever imagine.

Table of Contents

Foreword	8
Introduction	10
Chapter 1	15
Chapter 2	21
Chapter 3	27
Chapter 4	35
Chapter 5	43
Chapter 6	49
Chapter 7	55
Chapter 8	61
Chapter 9	67
Chapter 10	77
Chapter 11	83
Chapter 12	89
Chapter 13	95
Chapter 14	101
Chapter 15	107
Chapter 16	115
Chapter 17	123
Chapter 18	133
Chapter 19	141
Chapter 20	149
Summary	159

Foreword

I am a pastor and clinical therapist. I have taught in schools of theology and social work for a number of years. My first encounter with Carolyn was when she came to our church with her two little boys. She joined the church and volunteered to coordinate the nursery ministry. There was something in her eyes as I watched her grow over the years, serving in many capacities in the church. She ultimately completed her MSW and became a clinical social worker. She then went to seminary and was ordained by our church.

Carolyn tells of growing up in a world that seemed so strange to her. In this book she shares her stories. These stories are not mere historical accounts of her life. She takes you to the next level as she makes herself vulnerable and invites you into her life. This book takes you on a journey and will allow you to discover compassion, even for yourself, as the author allows you to travel with her as she seeks wholeness in body, mind, and spirit. Feel her emotions as you get in touch with your own.

You can sense her pain and celebrate her resilience as you enter into her sadness and joy, abandonment and grace, trauma and neglect, fear and shame. As human beings, many of us have felt some of the same sentiments that she has felt. Carolyn's stories matter and you will grow spiritually and emotionally as you read. As a clinician and spiritual leader, the author has developed new eyes and new enlightenment in her life, and gives of her best to her readers. Just as you watch her grow in the pages of this book, so will you.

Rev. Christine Y. Wiley
Ph.D., D. Min., MSW, LPC, LICSW, LCSW-Pastor Emerita, Covenant Baptist UCC, Washington DC, Adjunct Professor, Howard University School of Social Work, Washington DC

"Shout out to everyone who is out there trying to get through shit that they are not ready to share with others" - John Lewis aka Bad Ass Vegan.

Introduction

I grew up believing that there were only two types of girls –the "good" girls and the "bad" girls - and as I am typing this, I realize that the "bad" girls could actually be divided into two subcategories: the girls who could and liked to fight and the girls who slept around, were loose, hot and had no morals. I believed this because these were the messages that my community endorsed.

The reality is that, even today in this supposedly more enlightened time, our culture continues to place labels on females who express their sexuality in ways that we, as a society deem to be inappropriate. We are quick to judge; quick to stigmatize; quick to shame and demonize. We use terms such as whore, Jezebel, loose and THOT ("that ho over there"). We give them the "side eye," tell our sons to stay away from them and shake our heads in disapproval.

Every time I hear any of these terms, I tend to have a visceral reaction. What has caused me to react has changed over time but never the less, I still have a reaction. Each time a girl, and it is always a girl, is spoken of in negative terms because of her multiple sexual encounters, my first thought is "I wonder how old she was when she was first touched inappropriately?" "What was she exposed to - what did she see - what experience did she endure that has now shaped how she sees herself and her world?"

Why do these questions immediately come to mind for me? Probably because I was nine when I was first touched inappropriately and as I progressed through adolescence and young adulthood, I participated in all of the behaviors that would qualify me for all of the labels that tend to be assigned to "bad" girls.

As a teen, I was pretty much ambivalent about anyone's sexual behavior, including my own. It was the late 60's and the "sexual revolution was still in its prime, the pill was easily obtainable and HIV had not yet reared its ugly head. Folk were simply expressing themselves whenever and however they felt like it - well at least in some communities. As an adolescent, raised in the "Black Church" the consistent message was "wait until you are married - don't be a Jezebel." I heard this message on a regular basis, but the only effect it had on my behavior was for me to "do my thing" without getting caught. As I grew older, I justified my actions as setting my own standards and getting what I wanted on my own terms.

I firmly believed this until I was close to 30 years old and it finally dawned on me that maybe my sexual freedom was less a declaration of my dictating what was good for me and more an emotional response to having been repeatedly sexually molested for a number of years. Through therapy and reading other victims journeys, I learned that my sexual behavior was less "my choice" but rather my subconscious desire to erase the feelings of vulnerability that I became rooted in me as a result of the first time I was inappropriately touched.
Note: I am very clear that there are persons whose expression of their sexuality does come from a healthy place. Unfortunately, mine did not. Mine came from a place of confusion and a seeking of acceptance, and approval but for all the wrong reasons. Attempts to process my behaviors and feelings in therapy, while helpful, never really fully provided a space to process on the level I knew I needed. Even as the therapy sessions concluded, I still operated from the position of a sexual object. I still sought validation by using and or allowing my body to be used. It was only after multiple failed relationships, followed by intense self-examination, a lot of prayer and forgiveness (of myself and my

perpetrator(s) was I finally able to come to a place of self- acceptance, peace and wholeness.

My prayer is that this book will start you on a process so that you too can begin your journey of healing. This book is for young girls, women and anyone else who was introduced to sex before they were cognitively able to understand what was going on and as a result have indulged in behaviors labeled as inappropriate in desperate attempts to "reclaim" your power but to no avail.

If sexual abuse resulted in pushing you in the opposite direction – uncomfortable with sex, at war with your body and a distrust of anyone who tried to show you affection without any strings attached, I suspect you will also find parts of your journey in this book as well.

If you are ready to begin a path of healing so that you can have a healthy relationship with yourself and others, my prayer is that this book will help you to put into words those thoughts and feelings that we so skillfully attempt to ignore, try to hide or dismiss in our misguided attempts to protect ourselves. My prayer is that this book will give voice to your inner child - the one that was irrevocably harmed, and was without power and resources. If anything in this Introduction resonates with you, then, I encourage you to begin your path to healing by reading this book.

The format of this book is intentional. The title of each chapter begins with "The First Time…" and serves as a reminder that whatever was encountered or experienced happened more than once because "everything starts somewhere." Childhood abuse tends to result in unhealthy coping mechanisms and behaviors. As survivors, we might not have any clear idea about why we do what we do and, in many instances, we don't even want to do what we do, but yet we do it. This book will help the reader to recognize the unhealthy patterns and understand why survivors of childhood trauma "do what we do."

While the effects of childhood trauma can be devastating, healing can and does occur, if one is willing to commit to engaging in the healing process. While the work is not easy, trust me, the end results are well worth it. To assist in beginning the healing process, each Chapter ends with three questions. I encourage you to take time to "write" your responses. I am emphasizing the word "write" because your first instinct may be to just ignore the questions all together. I implore you to resist that urge and truly give yourself the gift of finally moving towards healing. In addition, answering the questions, allows you to move from simply reading the chapter(s) for entertainment to engaging the chapter from an introspective perspective. The activity of answering the questions as your responses relate to each individual chapter, will allow you to begin the much needed process of identifying your feelings/emotions, as well as begin to process them as oppose to either ignoring or simply willing the feeling/emotion to just go away. The third benefit of actively engaging the chapter(s) by responding to the questions is that it allows the reader to consider taking the next step of choosing to share those feelings/emotions that have surfaced. And trust me, this is a good thing because as scary as it might seem to share "the real you," it is that actually sharing that begins the process of healing and wholeness.

So, if you are still with me, at this point, then I suspect that something that you have read, thus far, has your interest. Something has begun to resonate with you. This is your time and this is your season to choose healing and wholeness. Thanks in advance for allowing me to share my path.

Chapter 1
The First Time…Stranger Danger

"About 1 in 5 black women have experienced rape in their lives & just under half of black women say they've experienced sexual violence." Sexual Abuse is defined by exposing a child to sexual material before they are cognitively able to process it.

Walking home, minding my business, don't remember what age but probably around 7 or 8. It was a time when kids could walk in the neighborhood without fear of being snatched. I had been walking to school alone since I had started school, gone to the store without adult supervision and explored the neighborhood, sometimes with my friends, but just as often alone.

As I walked down 27th Avenue, out of the corner of eye I notice a car - a car with a white man inside. This also wasn't unusual because although all of my neighbors were black, my class in school was predominantly filled with white children, my teacher was white, the man who ran the neighborhood store was white and Mom, my aunt's mother-in-law was white (or so I thought for the longest but actually she was just a very light complexioned woman from Kingston, Jamaica.

The point is that I lived in a bi-lateral world and the only significance white people had for me was that they existed in parts of my life but not all and I had learned early on to peacefully coexist with them in the specific areas where they showed up in my life. But back to the man in the car - I probably would have completely overlooked him, he probably would not have even been a dot on my radar, except that he beckoned to me to get my attention. He beckoned for me to come closer to the passenger side. Now I had not been taught about "stranger danger." I had not been taught that there are people in the world who mean you harm. I had not seen these images on the television that I could only selectively watch. I had not read about them in the newspaper because the only part of the paper I read was the comics. I just didn't know. What I had been taught was to respect my elders. What I had been taught was to try to be helpful and meet the needs of others. What I instinctively knew was that when an adult spoke, I was to listen or there would be hell to pay.

So when he beckoned me to come closer, I came closer - a little tentatively because I wasn't sure what he wanted, wasn't sure if I could help him, wasn't sure what was being asked of me. I came closer even though I had never experienced an adult who I did not know, sitting in a car a block away from my house trying to get my attention and much less asking me for anything.

As I came forward, I froze in my tracks. It felt like the air rapidly escaped my lungs and my eyes began to bulge. My heart began to race and momentarily I was frozen in place. While his face remained friendly, it was his hands that were grasping something pink and rapidly moving up and down. At the time, I did not have the words to understand what I was seeing, the cognitive ability to name what he was doing. All I knew was that the thing between his legs was red, and he was rapidly pulling it back and forth and his smile became a leer and his eyes took on an angry tone. And while I did not know what I was witnessing, I knew it was weird and wrong and I quickly turned and ran. And I never told anyone what I had seen but instead buried it in the recesses of my mind and I never really looked at white men the same again. Little did I know that this was only the first time...

Path to healing:

Which parts of this chapter do you relate to?

What emotion/feelings(s) are you currently experiencing?

If you are ready to share your feelings, at this time, who would you share them with?

What do you need to do to create the opportunity to share?

Chapter 2
The First Time - The Beginning

A baby girl, rejected by both mother and father, raised in different relatives households and a profound sense of not fitting in. Add in sexual molestation and exposure and what you have is a recipe for a train wreck - a train wreck that included promiscuity, hostage to fear, addiction and a profound sense of sadness and the determination to stay under the radar and maybe, just maybe I can find my "forever home."

There are three versions of my beginnings - two very dissimilar and two that are more closely aligned and no, they are not the same two. All of the versions agree that there was a "barmaid" who hooked up with a student at the Merchant Marine Academy. They all agree that their union resulted in a pregnancy. Two of the versions note that the paternal grandmother offered to "raise the baby" and those same two versions note that the new mother responded by saying "if she wants a baby, let her fuck and get one like I did." In both versions, the newly minted father then disappears and does not resurface until approximately 21 years later. And then there is his version where he denies even knowing that a baby had been born.

The saga continued with my mother bringing me home from the hospital and attempting to attend to her motherly duties. Now being a first time, mom can be a tremendous undertaking for most, but it was infinitely more challenging for my mother. Her pregnancy was not planned but rather was probably viewed as an unfortunate interruption. Bottom line, she was not prepared to be a mother. My birth was not a "blessed event." There was not a baby shower and there was probably minimal preparation but never-the-less, I was born and life drastically changed from what she had known. And yet, she made the decision to give motherhood a try. The first challenge was that I had colic and as a result, I cried a great deal.

Unfortunately, my mother could not tolerate my crying. She could not tolerate taking care of a child in distress. She could not tolerate the challenges of a new born and the colic definitely challenged her ability to be present in a loving way. So after two weeks of my crying and needing her attention, she called her sister and said "come and get this baby before I throw her out of the window." Thankfully my aunt came to her rescue and took me off of her hands and I would not live with my mother again (except for a brief period) until I was 15 years old. After a few years, I was sent to live with my grandparents until I was about 6 getting ready to turn 7 and starting the second grade. From the time I went to live with my aunt and then subsequent relatives, I had little contact with her. I simply didn't know this woman they had identified as my mother.

I didn't know this person who would send me toys at Christmas (and they would say that they came from Santa but I learned early on that she was Santa). I didn't know her, so imagine my surprise when she suddenly appeared and told me that I was going to be living with her in New York. I had no idea what to make of that. I was afraid and yet secretly pleased because I was going to be living with my mother and not with my aunt, or my grandparents, but my mother. I would no longer be the cousin who did not live with her own parents and yet I had no frame of reference of what this would be like, what would be expected, and what I would have to do so she did not send me away again. Well, that lasted all of about two months. It took her about two months to remember that she was not really cut out for the parenting thing. To remember that raising a child was more then she wanted to take on, so after some minor indiscretion or something (it didn't take much with her) I found myself back with my aunt again - without my mother. And yet, she was present in my live in a periphery kind of way. She would come drop off money to pay my aunt for taking care of me and then "visit" with me for about 10 minutes max.

Every Mother's Day and my birthday she would take me out for a meal and every now and then I would spend the night at her house and listen while she and her friends would drink, dance and have a good time. Her other way of spending time with me was when I would visit her would be to take me to "Eddie's Palm Garden" a bar where she hung out and as she socialized with her friends, I would sit in the back with the cook Clarence and eat whatever had been prepared. I lived for those visits. It was during those visits that I came to love the smell of a bar and alcohol and I couldn't wait to drink like her, dance like her and be the life of the party, just like her. I thought this was the most glamorous thing and vowed that when I got "big" I would be just like her. Everything starts somewhere. This was just the first time...

Path to healing:

Which parts of this chapter do you relate to?

What emotion/feelings(s) are you currently experiencing?

If you are ready to share your feelings, at this time, who would you share them with?

What do you need to do to create the opportunity to share?

Chapter 3
The First Time - Witnessing Family Dysfunction

If you have been reading this book from the beginning, you are probably going to struggle with my next sentence and with good reason because I have shared quite a number of things from my childhood that would lead one to surmise that life, definitely, "was not crystal staircase." And yet, it never really dawned on me that I came from a dysfunctional family until a few years ago. Yes, I was probably close to 20 before I finally realized that I had been molested repeatedly from age 9 to about 13. It had started when I was so young that I didn't have a name for it and I was always so taken off guard when it would occur again that I tried to pretend that it wasn't really happening. It took me a while to realize that both of my parents were alcoholics probably because their lifestyles seemed to be pretty normal to me. It took me a while to realize that growing up in a household with practicing heroin addicts was not quite the norm.

And while I knew that my family structure was not the traditional "mom, dad and 2.3 children, the idea that we could rightfully be labeled as dysfunctional never really occurred to me. Part of the reason is because I just naturally assumed that the things that were going on in my house were probably happening in others homes as well. The most I knew about my friends families was how they carried themselves in public - who knew what went on behind their closed doors. Truth be told, the only real models of family that I had direct access to observe were on television and while I loved shows like "Leave it to Beaver, Make Room for Daddy and Dennis the Menace" I knew that what was being portrayed did not look like my family. Besides the obvious racial difference, in my house there was no mother figure in my home who did not work but rather woke up, got dressed up to clean the house, cook dinner and greet "Dad" at the door when he came home from work. I knew that the challenges that "Beaver" had were not my story - his biggest issues appeared to be arguments with his brother or some minor infraction that resulted in a 'talk" from his dad. I don't remember any adult "talking" to me as a form of discipline. In my house, infractions were dealt with a whopping that frequently left scars and welts.

No, none of the family models that I saw on TV resembled my family nor even looked like me with the exception of "Julia" and that was still a leap as far as I was concerned. "Julia" starred Dianne Carroll as a single mom who was a nurse. While I could relate to the single mom aspect, I did not know anyone in my family who had a professional job like a nurse, instead my aunt worked in a factory and my mother worked in a bar and was a waitress at a lunch counter. So yes, you might say, I did not have any real models to compare my family structure against. I thought we were just like everyone else - with the exception that I lived with my aunt and not my parents. So imagine my surprise when I realized that in addition to substance abuse, molestation and abandonment, I had also been raised in a family that was affected by domestic violence.

I have no clear idea of my age but I know that I was young. All that I really remember is one night being herded into the basement, with my cousins, by my aunt's in-laws. I suspect that I might have been awakened from my sleep but I am not sure. What I do remember is either seeing my uncle with an axe or hearing someone saying that he is going after her with an axe. I don't remember what happened before that instigated the drama nor what happened afterward. All I know is that there were raised voices and a sense of urgency. And while I have no memory of any other acts of domestic violence, my adult- self suspects that this was not an isolated occurrence.

As I grew older I heard stories of how this same uncle would beat his children and then make then sit in a tub with cleanser which I can only imagine was extremely painful. This led me to be terrified of him because even at a young age, I understood this to be cruel. I remember an aunt sharing a memory of him in which she insists that while at the beach, he watched her struggle in the water (she said she was drowning) and he did not offer any assistance but instead just watched with a smirk on his face.

All of these messages led me to surmise that he was really not a nice person but again, it was only recently that I realized that his behavior made me a secondary victim to his display of domestic violence. Side note - soon after the axe situation, he announced that he had been "called to ministry" and left the family to attend seminary out of state. This was probably a blessing in disguise because I have no memory of him ever returning to live with us again.

What makes all of this pertinent is how I had, like so many of us, either ignored or normalized clearly dysfunctional behaviors within the family dynamic. I grew up during a time when you did not discuss family "business." I grew up during a time where the number one priority was to provide for your family. My aunt worked hard because I sincerely doubt that she was receiving any assistance from her husband and the amount my mom was giving her for my care was very little. So she worked, her full-time job in a factory and weekends babysitting little white children. More importantly, I grew up during a time where dysfunction and abuse were not really acknowledged - it was during the age when "spare the rod and spoil the child" was the prevailing thought and, in reference to domestic violence, many would equate the measure of a man with how well he "kept his woman in line." And yet, while no one necessarily agreed with any of these behaviors, they became family secrets that we just didn't talk about and definitely not in public.

As I mentioned earlier, it was just a few years ago that it finally dawned on me that while I had thought that my first trauma experience was the molestation, I had been exposed to traumatic stuff long before then as I suspect it was probably quite traumatizing to hear that your uncle is coming after your aunt with an axe. And as I type this, maybe there was an even earlier trauma going back to my being an infant that my mother decided she could not take care of. I have no idea what she may have done to "quiet that colicky baby" before she made the decision to call her sister and tell her to come and get me before, in her words, "I throw this baby out of the window.' Imagine growing up hearing this story on multiple occasions - I did and that was probably traumatizing as well.

All I know for sure is that there were a number of experiences from childhood beginning early on that led me to believe that the world was not a safe place, people are unpredictable, death could be imminent at any time and if I could just stay as quiet and as obedient as possible, someone could possibly really love me, protect me and make me feel safe. It would be years before I learned that "I was looking for love in all the wrong places. This was just the first time…

Path to healing:

Which parts of this chapter do you relate to?

What emotion/feelings(s) are you currently experiencing?

If you are ready to share your feelings, at this time, who would you share them with?

What do you need to do to create the opportunity to share?

Chapter 4
The First Time - "Off Balanced"

My earliest significant church memories were attending a Seventh Day Adventist church with my aunt and cousins. Being a Seventh Day Adventist was difficult for me for a number of reasons. First of all, we attended church on Saturdays, we called it the Sabbath and the Sabbath actually started on sun down Friday and lasted until sunset Saturday. We began the Sabbath (on Fridays) as a family with worship which included prayer and each person had to recite a bible verse.

My cousins and I would all try to go first so we could quickly say the shortest verse in the Bible "Jesus wept." Sometimes we were lucky, and sometimes we had to dig a little deeper and rattle off one of the versions of our next go to Scripture - the 23rd Psalm. Back then, Seventh Day Adventist were not only strict in observing the Sabbath, we also were not allowed to consume any products with caffeine, could not wear any jewelry, or wear makeup. It was well known that one didn't eat meat but if you did, you could only eat "clean" animals as mandated in Leviticus 11: NIV. "You may eat any animal that has a split hoof completely divided and that chews the cud." It is not clear to me why we were allowed to eat chicken, but thankfully we could. We could eat fish but not shrimp, crab or lobster. As a result, I remember thinking "when I grow up, I'm going to get a high school ring, wear earrings, drink a Coke or Pepsi and eat bacon!

Studying the Bible was very much encouraged so in addition to reciting our bible verse, we were also required to have completed our lessons for Sabbath School. Sabbath school took place before the main worship experience on Saturdays and you would not dare come to Sabbath school not prepared to discuss the lesson for the week.

Our church was in Harlem, we lived in Queens and my aunt did not have a car - as a matter of fact, I don't think she even knew how to drive. Most of the time, Sister Jones, my Aunt's choir director would give us a ride to church but when for whatever reason she was not available, we took the bus and train. One Sabbath Sister Jones was not available so we made the long trek on the subway and bus.

As we disembarked from the bus, I accidentally dropped my Sabbath School book. I had to be all of about 7 or 8 and all I knew was that there would be hell to pay if my Sabbath school book was either lost or damaged (or so I believed). As soon as I realized that the book had fallen by the buses back wheel, I reached down to retrieve it. Suddenly I felt myself being snatched by my collar and lifted off of my feet.

All I could hear was everyone hollering "what is wrong with you, you could have gotten run over." My eyes became as wide as saucers as I watched the enormous wheel of the bus run over the space I had just been reaching for and over my Sabbath School book. My heart was pounding for a number of reasons - I could have been run over because there is no way that the driver could have seen me.

My heart was pounding because everyone was yelling at me and I really could not understand why. Didn't they realize that I had to get my Sabbath School book? I felt like I was between a rock and a hard place and I couldn't comprehend what the "right" decision should have been. And although I wanted to cry as bad as I had ever wanted anything, my sense of confusion, shame and feeling uncomfortable prevented me from doing so.

I was confused because I thought I was doing the right thing by rescuing the book. Shame because I was being yelled at by my aunt and
both of my cousins and uncomfortable because I was now the center of attention and as I said earlier, my goal was to stay in the shadows as quiet as possible so that hopefully I could stay and not be moved yet again.

"Off Balanced" Again…

I was in elementary school about maybe 9 years old and one day I had walked to school as I usually did. This was something I usually did alone because that was just the way it was. It had been snowing pretty hard, but I didn't really notice because all I knew was that I was expected to go to school unless told otherwise and since I had not been told otherwise, off I went.

When I arrived there, there was no one there - which was odd. I had never encountered that before and I wasn't exactly sure what to do, but as I began to get colder, I decided to go back home. By the time I arrived home, the snow had begun to come down harder and the temperature had definitely dropped. As I approached the back door, I found that my hands had become so cold that I was having a hard time trying to manipulate my key (I was a latch key kid). Try as I might I just couldn't get my fingers to work - they were too cold. It never occurred to me to go to the front door and ring the bell because, in my mind, there was no one home. My aunt typically went to work just as I was awakening and my cousins, who were in junior high and high school, usually were also gone before me.

When I finally accepted the fact that my hands were too cold to manipulate the key and that I was not going to be able to unlock the door (I think my challenge was compounded because the lock itself had become frozen) it slowly began to occur to me that I was probably going to freeze to death and at this point I really didn't care. Suddenly I faintly heard someone calling my name from the other side of the door.

Now that was confusing in itself because I just knew that no one was home and the only living thing in the house was the cat who slept on the other side of the basement door and I knew that cats could not talk, much less call my name. When the door opened, I was greeted by my cousins who were laughing and loudly exclaiming "what are you doing out there - they closed schools because of the weather." I was so cold at this point that all I could do was just stand there and stare at them. The tears that I wanted to release were too cold to come out of my eyes.

How exactly was I to know that the schools had been closed due to the storm? Who would have told me? As I said, by the time I was awaked for school, everyone else had left the house to go to their respective places (work, and their schools). I typically got myself ready for school, fixed and ate my breakfast, washed my dishes, locked the house and walked to school.

Because I had gone about my regular routine of preparing and leaving for school, it never occurred to me to check my cousin's room to see if they were home and it would not have ever occurred to me to check the news for a "school closure" - this was New York City in the 60's - our schools is never closed unless there was a blizzard. So, in my mind, it was off to school I went, little knowing that the storm had developed into a blizzard and I unfortunately was caught outside in it. When my cousins realized that I really could not move, they guided me into the house and began the process of trying to thaw me out.

    As the sharp tingles that come when a body enters the warmth after having been exposed to bitter cold and begins to defrost, began to assault my fingers and toes, all I could think was here is yet one more time that I had felt like I had been left out of the loop - had not been given the right information, had been expected to "just know" things that I had no way of knowing. Once again, I felt uncared for and unprotected but instead of blaming them, I fell into my usual pattern of blaming myself and another piece of my non-existent self- confidence was chipped away. I wish I could say that "with time" those feelings simply went away, but that was not the case. The reality is that this was simply the first time...

Path to healing:

Which parts of this chapter do you relate to?

What emotion/feelings(s) are you currently experiencing?

If you are ready to share your feelings, at this time, who would you share them with?

What do you need to do to create the opportunity to share?

Chapter 5
The First Time - Touched Inappropriately

Home is where the heart is. There's no place like home. Home was supposed to be a place of sanctuary, a place of comfort, safety and warmth. A place of acceptance where you can let your hair down and not be on guard… just simply be.

I was approximately 9 years old and I know that it was morning because I still had on my pajamas. I was occupying myself in my room either playing with my dolls, listening to music on my portable record player or transistor radio or maybe even just reading a book (I have always loved reading since I read my first word at age 4 - "Mary-land.") A familiar voice called me into his bedroom and somehow or the other we began what I thought was the "tickle" game and tickling did occur, until…until I found myself on my back, my pajama bottoms had been pulled down and he was thrusting his penis in and out between my thighs.

I had absolutely no idea what was happening, all I knew was that it was he was bigger and stronger than me, his weight smothered me and it was no longer funny. And yet, I did not have the language to comprehend what was happening or why it was happening. All I knew was that it felt dark and scary and I was in a total state of shock. Shocked that this person who I looked up to had flipped the script and changed the game and it was no longer funny.

I didn't understand what was happening but when he finally stopped moving, no words were said. I was not acknowledged. I was sent back to my room and I felt scared, shocked and ashamed. Little did I know that these "attacks" would continue to occur for the next 3 -4 years until he found a new distraction - heroin.

The place of the molestation changed from his bedroom because I never went into that room again for years. The new place was the basement under the premise of hanging up the washed clothes. We were tasked to take the clothes to the laundry mat for washing but we would dry them on lines in the basement. At some point as we would hang up the clothes, some point which I could never predict. Some point that seemed to come out of the blue, I would find myself backed against the pool table, and the molestation would begin.

When a trauma occurs it tends to be remembered not in a linear fashion but rather in "bits and pieces." Flashes of his penis between my thighs, his mouth on my budding breasts that he would squeeze together to increase the size (I assume) and his voice instructing me to "squeeze your legs tighter, tighter." A sensation that caused my entire body to convulse and a wetness that smeared my thighs followed. No other words were ever spoken. No acknowledgement about what had happened - just silence. Silence and confusion on my part left me questioning if what had happened had actually happened or was it simply my imagination. The silence that would follow also fed my believe that I really didn't matter, that I was disposable and that I definitely had not control over my body and any say so of what could and could not be one to me. And if that wasn't enough, in spite of my fear and instinctive belief that what was happening was wrong (at 9 had no idea what sex (in any form), there was now and a new strange desire to recreate the "convulsion" down there because at least that part made me feel good, took me away (at least for a few minutes) from my present reality. Cognitively I had no language to explain or even identify what an orgasm was. All I know is that the "convulsion" made me feel wanted and less afraid, less dirty and less ashamed. And so I learned to create this "convulsion" on my own - I learned to masturbate. But try as I might to recreate this "good feeling" on my own, it never lasted longer than a few minutes. When I was finally able to catch my breath, shame, guilt and worthlessness would rapidly overtake me and the vicious cycle would continue. Needless to say, this "first time" set the stage for me viewing myself as a sexual object. This first time, because everything begins somewhere.

Path to healing:

Which parts of this chapter do you relate to?

What emotion/feelings(s) are you currently experiencing?

If you are ready to share your feelings, at this time with who would you share them?

What do you need to do to create the opportunity to share?

Chapter 6
The First Time - Lashing Out

When a child is sexually molested there are definitely behavioral changes. The most common behavioral change is anger which can be manifested as aggression (anger turned outward), and depression (anger turned inward). In my care, there were some of both. Not long after my mother determined, for the second time, that she could not deal with being a mother, I moved with my aunt. When my mother registered me for elementary school, it was determined that I qualified for what was called the "IGC" program - a program for "Intelligently Gifted Children."

As a result, even though I lived in a predominately black neighborhood and attended my neighborhood school, instead of us 'gifted" children being bused to a "better" school, white children were bussed to our neighborhood. From about the second grade through sixth grade, I was always one of about 5 black children in a class filled with children who did not look like me, did not live in my neighborhood and did not have my cultural experience and …my teachers were always white.

I was in probably the fourth grade and my teacher was preparing us for the upcoming awards assembly. By now my perpetrator had begun what I would later learn was molestation and I had become more withdrawn. My teacher explained that some students would be getting recognition for a number of things including good grades, perfect attendance, good citizenship, etc. As I listened to her explain what would occur, I felt my blood begin to boil. I don't know if I even raised my hand, but I do remember saying something about how I didn't think that it was fair that only some people would be recognized at the assembly. I spoke about the injustice of only honoring some while leaving others out. I don't remember all of what I said, but I do remember that when I finally stopped talking, everyone - the teacher and all of the students – were just staring at me. I have no idea what my teacher's response was because by this time my heart was beating so hard it felt like it was going to come right out of my chest. My skin began to flush with embarrassment and all I wanted to do was disappear. I could not believe that I had said anything. My pattern had been to stay as quiet as possible, follow the directions and do as I was told. Life had taught me to keep my feelings to myself and even better, don't feel at all.

It would be years before I would come to understand where the depths of my anger had come from. It had nothing to do with the guidelines of the recognition assembly, but rather it was intrinsically connected to the anger that I realized was always simmering, right beneath the surface as a result of the molestation that had taken over my life.

My teacher quickly had us line up and we proceeded to the assembly. Terror began to overtake me as I realized that my outburst had been completely out of line and I just knew that there would be a price to pay. Needless to say, I was flabbergasted when I was not dropped off at the office to be disciplined by the Principal. As we walked into the assembly, I tried to make myself as small as possible wishing that I could either take my words back or at the least, disappear. Imagine my surprise when my name was called multiple times as I was presented with multiple awards and recognitions. Unfortunately, I could not give myself permission to enjoy the honor and recognition because I had displaced my anger. All I could think about was how, yet one more time I had completely misread a situation and the one time when I decided to speak up, I had over-reacted. It would be years and many outbursts before I would come to understand how destructive anger can be for persons who have sustained a trauma. This was just the first time...

Path to healing:

Which parts of this chapter do you relate to?

What emotion/feelings(s) are you currently experiencing?

If you are ready to share your feelings, at this time, who would you share them with?

What do you need to do to create the opportunity to share?

Chapter 7
The First Time – Nightmares

One of the symptoms that might manifest as a result of someone sustaining a trauma is nightmares/night terrors. For many, the content of the dream(s) might be directly based on parts of the actual trauma, but for children who have been sexually traumatized, because of their lack of full cognitive understanding of what has occurred, the dreams may be more metaphorical in nature.

I grew up watching what I will call "scary" movies. Unlike today where there may be multiple televisions in a home and or multiple devices in which one can stream whatever content you might desire, in my aunt's home there was only one television which resided in the living room. As a result, unless I was watching TV alone, I had little choice in what in what the folk who were older and bigger and stronger than me might want to watch and they loved "scary" programs. During the 1960's, it felt like there was no end of "scary" programs to choose from. There was "Chiller Theater," "The Twilight Zone" and "The Outer Limits" to name a few. There were movies like "The 50 Foot Women" and "House on a Haunted Hill." And of course, there was the King Kong, Godzilla movies to boot. All of them scared me to know end, but that did not stop me from watching - my cousins were gathered around the television and I didn't want to be left out.

I guess my desire to fit in, to be a part of, overrode my fear. Out of all of these shows/movies, the one movie that made the biggest impression was King Kong. I was completely fascinated with the original King Kong movie (you know the one with Fay Raye and although Jessica Lange did a great job in the remake of the movie, it was the original version that completely captured my imagination).

Each time I watched it, and I watched it multiple times. I would literally shake in my boots especially during the part where King Kong begins to destroy the train. I grew up in New York City and in my mind because they had captured King Kong and brought him to Manhattan, and because the train that he grabs and shakes was an elevated line, I believed in the depths of my very soul that the train was the same Number 7 line that we would ride to go to church, and this belief sent my anxiety through the roof.

The only thing that probably prevented me from going into a full blown panic attack was because we never really rode the train at night and King Kong was destroying trains and stuff at night (at least that was my logic).

While I didn't really think that an ape could grow to be that large, there was still a part of me that wondered ...well, maybe it could happen. I mean, wasn't Kong the "eighth wonder of the world?" So, I really couldn't be totally sure that apes that big did not exist.

When the molestation started I began to have nightmares about King Kong. From a metaphorical sense, King Kong represented a figure that was significantly bigger and stronger than me. King Kong could, at times, be likable but could also be uncontrollable and strike fear in my heart - all qualities of my perpetrator. There were basically two nightmares that I would repeatedly experience. In one variation King Kong would be peering through my window (just like he had done in the movie while looking for Faye Raye). In the nightmare, I would be so paralyzed with fear that I couldn't cry out, and I couldn't get off the bed. All I could do was try to hold myself as rigid as possible bracing myself for whatever was to follow - which was exactly what I would do and feel each time I found myself being molested. In another variation of the nightmare, I would be at my school's playground on, believe it or not, the "monkey bars." King Kong would again be advancing towards me and again, I was frozen in place petrified with fear. In the nightmares, King Kong never actually touched me, but the fear that I experienced contributed to what I later learned was increased anxiety.

I began to grind my teeth at night and at times, the fear would continue even after I awaken. I became fearful of just about everything - fearful that I would be hurt or harmed. As a result, this fear directed my ongoing goal which was to try to stay as safe as possible even if it limited my interactions and caused me to be too fearful to engage in "fun" activities simply because I was concerned about my safety. For the most part, my self- imposed precautions worked I limited my interactions and became a voracious reader because as I entered into the lives of the stories in the books, I felt safe. The problem is that I couldn't find a place to be safe from my perpetrator, who unlike King Kong actually did touch me. And I wish I could say that this dream only occurred once, but unfortunately, it was only the first time…

Path to healing:

Which parts of this chapter do you relate to?

What emotion/feelings(s) are you currently experiencing?

If you are ready to share your feelings, at this time, who would you share them with?

What do you need to do to create the opportunity to share?

Chapter 8
The First Time - I Self Medicated

My first time trying illicit drugs was in my early adolescence. My cousin had given me a joint of "reefer" which I shared with a friend. I don't remember choking probably because I had already started to sneak and smoke cigarettes.

What I do remember is getting a feeling that blissfully took me out of my reality (molestation and living with two practicing heroin addicts). I loved everything about "getting high" and quickly began to experiment with everything I could get my hands to recreate that feeling.

My friend Rhonda was from a large family of 8 and there were always good times to be had at her house. Her father had a great big station wagon and he would pile all of the neighborhood kids in it and take us to the pool, the drive in and other fun places. It was on one of these excursions that I first heard a group that I initially thought was the "5 Stair Steps", but turned out to be the Jackson 5. In this car, I could experience "normal childhood things. My aunt was always too busy working to take us any place other than church. Mine was not a life of dance or piano lessons or even after school activities.

The only outings I remember doing with my aunt, other than visiting family, was when she would occasionally take me to her babysitting jobs that she did to augment her wages as a factory worker. (she would babysit for a Jewish family in Forest Hills, so instead of the kids coming to her, we went to them). So I looked forward to spending time with my friend's family - there was always something to do, somewhere to go and her father seemed to actually like doing things with us.

He was a really cool guy, but what I initially didn't realize was that most of the time he was with us, he had been drinking. Eventually, I am assuming his drinking became a problem because the next thing we knew he had been given "medication" to stop him from drinking. Well, this intrigued us.

We had tried "reefer" and loved it, so we decided that whatever he was taking probably was even better than smoking a joint. So my friend stole some of his pills and we took them - anything to change our moods. This did not go well because my friend got sick (I think she took more than me) and our secret was out - we were caught and my aunt tore my behind up, but that did not stop me. I like the feeling of getting high and thus began an approximate 16 year journey of taking anything I could get my hands on if I believed it would get me high and take the edges off of my reality.

The only drug I never tried was heroin and that was primarily because I do not like needles and secondarily because I would hold the belt for one of my cousins when he would get high so he could "hit" himself. Watching him cook the heroin up, inject it in his veins and then subsequently nod off was horrifying to me, but each time he would tell me to hold the belt, I would. Being molested on an ongoing basis had taught me to be compliant even when everything in me silently screamed "no."

The reality was that I had no idea that I could say no - I had yet to find my voice. Looking back, I am grateful that I had not been offered heroin. I am grateful that I disliked needles and I am eternally grateful that when my other cousin began what would turn out to be a lifelong love of "smack", he stopped molesting me.

What I did develop from my own drug use was an addiction that almost cost me everything, but for the grace of God, a Sponsor and 12-step rooms with guiding principles and people who loved me until I could learn to love myself. Addictions all start somewhere this was simply the first time…

Path to healing:

Which parts of this chapter do you relate to?

What emotion/feelings(s) are you currently experiencing?

If you are ready to share your feelings, at this time, who would you share them with?

What do you need to do to create the opportunity to share?

Chapter 9
The First Time…Bottom Line – Foundation

My relationship with my mother was pretty much always challenging to say the least. To recap from previous chapters, before being politically correct came into fashion, my birth was described as illegitimate because my parents were not married. If the truth be told, I don't even think they were a couple at this point. I honestly have no idea what this may have been like for her but I suspect that my birth was not viewed as a blessed event.

After my birth when my father and his cousin relayed my grandmother's request that she be given "the child" (me) to raise, my mother's response was "tell her to fuck and get one like I did." I would love to romanticize this by believing that she had loved me so much that the idea of someone else raising me was out of the question, but alas, that was not the case because not too long after she brought me home, she called my aunt and told her to "come and get this crying baby before I throw her out of the window."

Growing up I only saw my mother sporadically - when I was with her parents, I don't remember visiting at all except when she came to bring me back to New York with her. This living arrangement was short lived and after a few months, I went to live, again, with my aunt. While I was there, my mother would come by once a week primarily to drop off the money she was giving my aunt for my care. Her visits would last no longer than 15 minutes tops and then she would be gone again until next week. Every now and then I would spend the night at her house primarily in her room while she entertained her friends in the living area. Up until my teen years, I don't remember her necessarily being mean, she was merely absent enough that I really didn't know her nor she know me.

When I was 15 I returned to live with her, this time in Washington, DC and from my perspective it was pretty cool because she pretty much let me do whatever I wanted - I could smoke cigarettes in front of her, I could hang out without a curfew and she provided my basic needs. But again, there was little direct interaction between us. She had her own way of thinking and doing things and as long as I didn't stop her flow, there was a sense of peace. But when her flow was interrupted…I got to see a whole different side. She would get so angry that she would swear that she "would see red." She would curse the offender out assassinating the offender's character, and no, she was not above name calling.

For her, when she got mad, it was "anything goes." I noticed that when she became a grandmother, her demeanor (at least towards her grandchildren) became less abrasive and more loving and kind and if she did "kirk out" about something in their presence, she would say "I'm sorry baby" - words she never said to me. One day when the boys were young, we had driven to New York to visit her. I had recently purchased my first brand new car and was still learning all of the intricacies of how it operated. A friend helped drove up with us to New York to visit her family and on the way back to Maryland we decided to stop at Inner Harbor. When we returned to the car, we quickly realized that our luggage that had been in the trunk of the car was gone - they had been stolen. I had not known that the trunk did not automatically lock so while the car itself had been secured, the trunk had not. I was devastated. I felt violated and angry because my boy's suitcases were full of new clothes I had just purchased in New York and I had no idea how I was going to replace those clothes. I also felt embarrassed because my friend's luggage had also been taken as well and when I realized my erroneous thinking about the trunk, I became overcome with guilt and I couldn't figure out a way to replace her things because, again, I had spent all of my money (and in those days, every penny was carefully accounted for).

My friend was very supportive, and repeatedly told me not to worry about it. When I dropped her off at her place, she allowed me to use her phone to call my mother and tell her what had happened (this was way before the days of cell phones). After hearing my recitation about what I had just experienced, my mother response was to curse me out telling me that I was stupid, that it was all my fault and that I should have known better… better yet, that I should not have stopped at all.

While my friend could not hear this conversation between my mother and myself, she could see my face and when the call was ended, she offered me a drink. Now I was probably less than a few years in sobriety and every fiber in my being wanted to scream "yes". I had not shared with my friend my substance abuse history so she didn't know the magnitude her offer held. My mind quickly calculated, I just got robbed and cursed out. From my way of thinking, I definitely deserved a drink… one drink couldn't hurt or could it? I mean, alcohol had always been there for me. If I was happy, I would celebrate with a drink or a joint or something. If things were not going well, getting high always helped to reduce the tension I might have been experiencing. In my mind, if any occasion could justify a drink, this one definitely qualified. But somewhere in the back of my mind, I remember a phrase that I often heard in meetings "One is too many and a thousand never enough." For me this meant that my drinking had long gone past the phase of being able to be satisfied with "just one." Having more than one, tended to not end well, so while my mind was screaming "yes, give me that drink in a big glass thank you" the words that came out of my mouth were "No."

The next day, I made my way to a 12 step meeting and shared what I had experienced. As usual, after I had finished sharing, the group said "keep coming back." But when the meeting ended, after the Serenity and the Lord's Prayer were recited, and as hugs were being given, people began to press money into my hands, At first I couldn't fully comprehend what was happening but when it dawned on me the level of love this group of recovery alcoholics were demonstrating towards me, I became overwhelmed - I was not been criticized, I was being shown support and love from people who didn't have to do either. From people who were struggling just like me to live life on life's terms, people who openly cared about me, just because.

Sometime later, I was chatting with my Sponsor and complaining about my mother questioning if she even liked me. My Sponsor quietly listened and then said "Just suppose your mother really doesn't like you." I remember looking at the phone because I couldn't believe that she had just said that. She repeated her statement again, "Just suppose your mother really doesn't like you." This time, I began to cry, and cry, and cry. It felt like the flood gates had been opened as I cried an ugly, howling cry that felt like it was coming from the depths of my soul. My Sponsor never said a word but patiently waited. When my tears had finally subsided and I could catch my breath, she repeated her statement a third time "Just suppose your mother really doesn't like you." This time, instead of me crying, I slowly began to feel as if a weight had been lifted from my chest. I realized that because I had spent most of my life trying to get my mother to treat me better or at least interact with me on more than a superficial level, I had internalized the belief that there must be something I had done or needed to do to become loved or at minimum be found acceptable by my mother.

This belief has definitely impacted how I interacted with others or choose not to interact with others because in my mind, if I was not acceptable to my mother - the one who had carried me for 9 months and given me life then how could I possibly be acceptable or loved by anyone else. And while on one level I had internalized that I was unlovable, on another level I was hoping that this wasn't true. But if in fact my mother really didn't like me, then I now had the freedom to stop trying to gain her affection.

After I shared this with my Sponsor, she responded by reading me the Psalm 139:

1 You have searched me, Lord, and you know me. 2 You know when I sit and when I rise; you perceive my thoughts from afar. 3 You discern my going out and my lying down; you are familiar with all my ways. 4 Before a word is on my tongue you, Lord, know it completely. 5 You hem me in behind and before, and you lay your hand upon me. 6 Such knowledge is too wonderful for me, too lofty for me to attain.

7 Where can I go from your Spirit? Where can I flee from your presence? 8 If I go up to the heavens, you are there; if I make my bed in the depths, you are there. 9 If I rise on the wings of the dawn, if I settle on the far side of the sea, 10 even there your hand will guide me, your right hand will hold me fast. 11 If I say, "Surely the darkness will hide me and the light become night around me," 12 even the darkness will not be dark to you; the night will shine like the day, for darkness is as light to you. 13 For you created my inmost being; you knit me together in my mother's womb. 14 I praise you because I am fearfully and wonderfully made; your works are wonderful, I know that full well. 15 My frame was not hidden from you when I was made in the secret place, when I was woven together in the depths of the earth. 16 Your eyes saw my unformed body; all the days ordained for me were written in your book before one of them came to be. 17 How precious to me are your thoughts,[a] God! How vast is the sum of them! 18 Were I to count them, they would outnumber the grains of sand— when I awake, I am still with you. 19 If only you, God, would slay the wicked! Away from me, you who are bloodthirsty! 20 They speak of you with evil intent; your adversaries misuse your name. 21 Do I not hate those who hate you, Lord, and abhor those who are in rebellion against you? 22 I have nothing but hatred for them; I count them my enemies. 23 Search me, God, and know my heart; test me and know my anxious thoughts. 24 See if there is any offensive way in me, and lead me in the way everlasting.

She then told me to focus on verse 13-16 and bid me good night. These verses became my bottom line. If God said that

I am fearfully and wonderfully made, that God knew me even when I was yet in my mother's womb, if God knows everything about me and still loves me, then that was something to shout about, something to get excited about, something that would become the new foundation for my life and my interactions with others. The first time...

Path to healing:

Which parts of this chapter do you relate to?

What emotion/feelings(s) are you currently experiencing?

If you are ready to share your feelings, at this time, who would you share them with?

What do you need to do to create the opportunity to share?

Chapter 10
The First Time - Using My Voice

I was raised during the era of "children should be seen and not heard." On top of this, as a child who always felt that I never really fit in, who was not a part of a family unit (I.e. mother, father, sister, brother), my goal in life was to try to stay as quiet as possible, as obedient as possible and outside the radar so that maybe, just maybe, I could call somewhere home and not be shipped off to live with yet another somebody.

I read a lot, played by myself a great deal of the time hoping that I wouldn't get noticed and yet secretly wanting to be noticed. This worked, for the most part and I only changed households a total of five times and two households I lived in twice each. When I would get in trouble and asked "why did you do that?" The fear that I would be moved would keep me from answering. If someone asked me if I liked something or wanted something, for the most part I would simply shrug my shoulders and accept whatever was decided for me.

If I was happy, mad, sad, anxious, nervous whatever emotion I was feeling, I kept to myself because in addition to being afraid of being "put out" I also firmly believed that no one cared, so I kept it to myself. I remember as a teen when I had returned to living with my mother an incident that happened when I took a risk and said how I felt. It was a Sunday afternoon and the extended family would gather at my grandfather's home (where my mom and I were living) after church for Sunday dinner and visiting. I remember leaning against the screen door and the glass fell out and shattered. My mother began to berate me as only she could, using expletives and colorful language worthy of any sailor. Basically, she cursed me out. Her words made me feel so small and insignificant. Her words questioned my worth and my very existence. To say that I was embarrassed was an understatement because this occurred in front of all of my extended relatives. Yes, I was embarrassed but I was also deeply hurt and angry. Suddenly, I spoke my mind. I would have thoughts in response to how I was treated or experienced things but never would I speak them out loud. But this time, I was done and the thought became words spoken out loud and I said "I didn't ask to be born." I had finally taken a risk and spoke up for myself only to have my mother quickly reply "if abortions had of been legally you wouldn't have been."

All that I could do was stare, her words hurt more than if she were to have struck me. The weight of the enormity of her words fell on me and all I felt was dumb struck for I don't know how long. There was never any discussion about this, never an apology, never any sign or demonstration of remorse. What did happen was that it reinforced my belief that I didn't matter.

Fast forward about two years later and I was on my way to the airport to begin a summer program before my freshman year of college. My aunt was driving me. She was the aunt who was comfortable with silence; the aunt who radiated warmth by simply being present. As we quietly rode to the airport for what would be my first time living away from family and also my first plane ride, I began to feel a knot of anxiety building up inside of me. Accompanying the anxiety was a growing sense of fear and I took the risk and barely whispered "just suppose they don't like me." Even as I type this, tears are beginning to well up in my eyes as if it was yesterday. That old familiar feeling of possibly not being good enough began to overtake me - "just suppose they don't like me." I am sure my aunt had to ask me to repeat what I had just said because I had said it so softly. I don't remember what her response was, but what I know is that it was loving and kind and most importantly demonstrated that she was listening to me - that what I had to say mattered. Whatever she said reassured me that my feelings were valid and more importantly that it was going to be alright. That was the first time I intentionally shared my feelings.

Path to healing:

Which parts of this chapter do you relate to?

What emotion/feelings(s) are you currently experiencing?

If you are ready to share your feelings, at this time, who would you share them with?

What do you need to do to create the opportunity to share?

Chapter 11
The First Time - Black Out

I loved everything about getting high. I loved the taste of alcohol, the tinted haze of marijuana, the adrenaline rush of cocaine and the altered universe of hallucinogenic drugs. From my first joint, in my opinion, I came to believe that everything was better if you were at least buzzed. In that altered state, the world appeared kinder and gentler, I didn't have to worry about fitting in and the bad memories could remain safely in the background. Did I mention that I was also a bookworm who loved reading as much as getting wasted because reading also transformed me to places were my own guilt, shame and fear did not reside.

By the time I was applying to go to college I knew there were a few places I dared not go because I knew the drugs would definitely get me off the academic path and I had to maintain my good girl/bad girl persona. As a result I avoided schools in California because they were getting "lit" out there and I knew that would probably be my destruction.

The school I ultimately chose was in the middle of nowhere and that was fine by me because I figured it might help me to stay focused and being awarded a full scholarship was definitely a motivating factor. Little did I know that wherever I went, I was taking myself with me and that included my love affair with drugs and alcohol. Not long after I hit the campus, I quickly connected with the folk who liked what I liked and were willing to provide it in abundance. And when drugs were not necessarily as accessible as I would have liked (I was a scholarship student with limited funds), I was able to purchase alcohol and, believe it or not, have it delivered to the dorm.

During my junior year, I had an experience that totally perplexed me and that I struggled to understand. I had gone to a club and was sitting at the bar having a few drinks. My next memory was waking up in my bed. To say I was shocked would be an understatement. Let's see, I remembered sitting at the bar, I remembered drinking but I had no memory of how I went from that bar stool to waking up in my bed. I remember kind of holding my breath to see if I could hear someone else in my small apartment - but all was quiet. I slowly checked to see if I was naked or clothed and if clothed, did I have on pajamas or street clothes or some combination of the two. It turns out that I was fully clothed in what I had worn the night before. I checked to see if there were any signs that someone had been with me in the apartment and maybe had left while I was asleep - it didn't appear so.

I checked to see if my door was locked (it was) and while I found my keys, my purse was missing. As I was doing all of this "checking" what bothered me the most was that I did not remember anything between sitting at the bar and waking up in my bed. I wanted to call the person who I had been out with to try to figure out what had happened, but I couldn't figure out how to ask - I couldn't tell them that I did not remember because that would make me…I don't know how it would have made me but I knew it could not be good. So I called the club and inquired if they had found my purse, and they were kind enough to search the area where I had been seated. They actually found it under a table that I had no memory of sitting at – so the plot thickened. They assured me that it looked like everything was intact and agreed to secure it until I could come to retrieve it.

I finally called my friend and pretended as if I was not terrified that I was possibly losing my mind. I was like "we had a good time last night" and kept trying to make statements that would prompt my friend to divulge if I had passed out, cut up or what. Apparently, nothing seemed out of the ordinary to them and after a few more minutes, I ended the call as confused as ever. I made the decision to simply pretend like it had never happened. It would be years later before I would come to understand that what I had experienced was the first of many alcoholic blackouts. This was simply the first time...

Path to healing:

Which parts of this chapter do you relate to?

What emotion/feelings(s) are you currently experiencing?

If you are ready to share your feelings, at this time, who would you share them with?

What do you need to do to create the opportunity to share?

Chapter 12
The First Time - I Betrayed a Sister

One of the results of having been sexually molested as a child (being exposed to sexual activity/things, etc. before you are cognitively able to process it) is that you either become overly sexualized or under sexualized. I bet you can't guess which persona I took on! For years I had no real idea what a healthy sexual relationship was or looked like.
Furthermore, whatever it was I wasn't interested. I wasn't interested in being in a relationship, I wasn't interested in commitment. What I was interested in was replacing the emotional detachment and depression I often felt with the "feel good" body sensations that being with a male, for the most part would bring. In my mind, I was in control of my body, I pursued and got what I wanted and even if it wasn't exactly what I wanted, I convinced myself that it was.
Being in control was extremely important to me because during the years of my molestation, I was being controlled. I was being used when and where my perpetrator felt like it without my consent, without any preamble and always ending in silence. Somewhere deep down I understood that my body had some kind of power - exactly what, I had no idea but it must have had power because it was what the guys wanted and would go to great lengths to get. So I became over sexualized in an interesting kind of way.
I always teetered between dressing chaste and somewhat provocative. During my adolescence I wore a 36-C bra and weighed about 120 pounds.
At 5'7, my breasts kind of just jumped out at you - they were the first things most people noticed. And while that attention

did make me feel uncomfortable (I'm an introvert at heart) it also boosted my false sense of believing that I was in control. So yes, I had my share and more of sexual partners and exploits but if the guy began "to catch feelings", I would find a way to "ease on down the road" - I did not want a commitment or a relationship. I did not "want to go with you" and no, you could not "have a chance." (My DMV folks will know what that means).

Now that is not to say that I did not have morals or some sort of boundaries. I did. They were just a bit interesting. Everyone has a bottom line that guides their behavior. Something that is absolutely verboten for them. My bottom line was that I would not get involved with a married man. Have I flirted a little bit with married men? Yes, some times. Have I secretly wanted to check out a married man? You betcha I did but the reality is that I did not. That was my bottom line and I have always stuck with that. My other code is that I would not "mess around" with the boyfriend(s) of my friends - they were off limits, well sort of. The sort of was if the guy was dating a friend of mine - then hands off, but, if they hadn't exactly started dating yet, then let's say that might be a different story and thus the topic of this chapter. The first time I betrayed a friend was when she confided in me that she liked one of the brothers on campus. I hadn't really thought about him one way or the other and my intention was to help her in her pursuit of him. During my college days, we spent a great deal of time playing Bid Whist and smoking weed. After she expressed her interest in him, I began to chat with him about my friend with the intention of parking his interest in her. My intentions were good - my goal really had been to let him know that she was interested in him and hopefully spark his interest in her. To say that it didn't turn out that way is an understatement. He quickly honed in on me, and began his "full court press" in pursuit of me. I was like a deer caught in the head lights. All thoughts of my friend somehow went out the window and I began to respond to the attention he was showing me. Needless to say, before long we became involved and I didn't even have the grace to feel bad. I had betrayed a friend and miraculously, she remained my friend even though I don't understand why.

Years later, after some therapy, I finally understood that what I had done was foul - I had broken the "unwritten" code amongst friends that identifies the category of potential partners that are off limits. And which category is this? Well, simply put anyone your friends either have previously dated or had been previously interested in. Unfortunately, it would take me years to fully understand and until I did, this was definitely the first time ...but not the last.

Path to healing:

Which parts of this chapter do you relate to?

What emotion/feelings(s) are you currently experiencing?

If you are ready to share your feelings, at this time, who would you share them with?

What do you need to do to create the opportunity to share?

Chapter 13
The First Time - I Met My Father

I did not meet my father until I was 20 years old. As mentioned earlier, I only had spent brief periods of time living with my mother (with the exception of my second attempt at high school which is a whole other chapter.) All of my life I had been told the following things about my father - His name, where he was from (Boston), his nationality - Jamaican or as my mother would say "an arrogant Indian." I was also constantly reminded, by my mother, that I was smart like him and that should have been a compliment except when she would say it, it felt more like another deficiency "you smart just like your father that arrogant West Indian." As a little girl, I would create intricate fantasies about my life. In my fantasies, my life was infinitely better and they all included my father.

Back then catalogs were big. They arrived to my aunt's home on a pretty regular basis because apparently my aunt ordered a number of their garments. I would spend hours raving over these catalogs picking out the clothes I would wear in my fantasy life with my made up family. In this family was a father/husband and brothers/sons but never a mother. As a matter of fact, depending on which day I was fantasizing, I was sometimes the mother and sometimes the daughter. When I say I spent hours doing this, I do mean hours. I would pick out clothes for everyone for every occasion. I would pick out the appliances for our fantasy home making sure I had accounted for every detail. I didn't have a face in mind for this father/husband figure - I didn't need one. All I knew was that he was there and I felt safe, loved and cared for. These bouts of fantasy continued until the molestation began and, just like that the fantasy was no more - my world had been irrevocably disrupted and even my fantasy life no longer felt safe.

Fast forward to my college years...I had a work-study job with the EPA and my boss was a black man. He and his wife befriended me and I would sometimes babysit their children in addition to my work-study responsibilities. At work, he would ask me about my family and when he learned that I had never met my father, his curiosity peaked. One day he asked me what did I know about my father, so I told him all that I knew. He began to dial the phone and a few seconds later I heard him say my father's name and ask for his telephone number. He then wrote the number on a piece of paper and completed his call. I asked me if I wanted to make the call, but all I could do was look at him completely dumbfounded. I had momentarily lost the power to speak.

I was staring at him like he had two heads. I could not believe what he had done. I was scared and nervous and felt like I had been ambushed. But I was also surprised that all it took to possibly get my father's phone number was to call the operator - why had this never occurred to me before. I must have shaken my head "no" that I was not able to make the call, because he simply began to dial those numbers himself. As I watched him, I realized that my heart was pounding as if it was outside of my chest.

A part of me wanted to reach over and slam the phone down but a greater part of me wanted to see this thing through – could this be possible, could my fantasy become real? Someone must have answered the phone because my boss asked for my father. A few seconds later, he said "hold on" and handed me the phone. I gulped and asked a series of questions, holding my breath between each of his answers. "Were you in the Merchant Marine Academy?" He responded "Yes." Did you know a woman named Odell Johnson" and without hesitation or pause, he responded "yes." I then paused and before my courage left me, I said "then I guess you are my father." He paused and then quickly asked where I was and told that he would be booking a flight and coming to see me the next day. I prayed that he was telling the truth but was afraid to fully believe it.

When I got home, I told my roommate Pat what had happened and she quickly offered to drive me to the airport the next evening to meet his plane. The next day we arrived at the airport and proceeded to the gate (this was back in the days prior to 9/11 when you could greet passengers at the gate). When the flight landed, I anxiously waited, having no idea what he looked like and realizing he also had no idea what I looked like as well. Pat was trying to calm my anxiety and fears but she was equally excited about what was about to unfold. We watched as the passengers came through the hallway off of the plane and I surveyed every face looking for an African American man who might possibly look like me.

As the swarm of people began to trickle down, I could feel a wave of disappointment begin to overtake me - I thought, "He didn't come". All of a sudden a tall very erect man appeared, walking with purpose. Pat was so excited that she ran up to him and grabbed him and hugged him. Even as he hugged her back, his eyes found mine - I was literally frozen in place. As she released him, very slowly we walked towards each other and that was the first time that I met my father.

Path to healing:

Which parts of this chapter do you relate to?

What emotion/feelings(s) are you currently experiencing?

If you are ready to share your feelings, at this time, who would you share them with?

What do you need to do to create the opportunity to share?

Chapter 14
The First Time - Birthday Party

I was living in Boston after reconnecting with my father. It was my 25th birthday and I was feeling a little down because my plans to hang out with a friend had been delayed due to a celebration her job was having for her boss who also shared the same birthday as me. Needless to say, I was feeling some kind of way because here she was celebrating her boss's birthday and no one was celebrating with me.

I was in my feelings because first of all whenever she did appear, it was just going to be us, because our other friends had plans, were busy, doing something else...I don't know what but what I knew was that those old feelings of abandonment was creeping in. This was starting to look like not much of a birthday celebration.

As I began to settle into my pity party, I noticed a note on my car windshield. This was long before the days of cell phones so communication was not as easy as it is today. The note was from her apologizing for delay and adding that she would be with me shortly. She ended by adding "Happy birthday Jimmy Carter." The back story is that my friend, when she first heard the date of my birthday would always said "you have the same birthday as Jimmy Carter" - hence the note.

Eventually we met up and she then said, before we celebrate your birthday, I need to stop by Paula's house to pick something up. "Stop at Paula's house and pick something up?" Now I was confused and moving from feeling sorry for myself to feeling annoyed, but nevertheless, off to Paula's we went. When we got to Paula's, as I walked into her home I noticed that her house was decorated with party stuff and there was even a cake on the table. As I exclaimed, "look at this cake and all of these decorations, Paula must be having a party for someone and she didn't even invite me." Suddenly, in the middle of my rant, something clicked. The pieces came together - the cake, decorations, friends were all smiling at me. It finally dawned on me that the party was for me.

You could have bought me for a penny. People began to come out of the other rooms laughing and shouting "Happy Birthday." To say that I was stunned would be an understatement. I was stunned, overwhelmed, surprised and somewhat shocked because I had never had a party of any kind, much less a birthday party! I was 25 years old and never had a party before.

As I was trying to process this, someone put a glass with (at the time) my favorite drink in it and again, I was surprised because they remembered! And we began to do toasts with ice cold vodka, no chaser because how else do you drink Stolichnaya? I wish I could say that it was a nice party. I wish I could relate funny stories about the festivities, the cutting of the beautiful cake or the food that was eaten. I wish I could, but the reality was the last thing that I remembered was drinking after each toast.

My next memory was waking up in a bed and having no idea where I was. It slowly began to dawn on me that I was probably at Paula's house and as soon as that realization hit me, I quickly checked to see what my state of dress or undress was. A quick check reassured me that I had all of my clothes on so I could eliminate at least one possibility of what had occurred. This was not my first alcohol induced blackout - that had happened in college where the scenario was almost the same as this time except my last memory then had been in a bar and when I awoke, I was in my own bed thankfully alone and fully clothed. I didn't know that what I had experienced was called a black out. What I knew was that just like that time in college, this time I would have to depend on others to fill in the blank because I sure as hell could not. But the question is always, how do you find out what happened? How do you fill in the blanks without admitting that you have no memory? Thankfully, my friend called and through her laughter, somewhat filled me in on what had transpired.

Clearly I had gotten too drunk to drive home so I was put to bed. After the fog cleared, because yes, I did have a hangover, once I could sit up without feeling sick to my stomach, once I got home and began to reflect on how my friends had definitely surprised me, once I realized how much my friends thought of me, I could finally smile and reflect on what I could remember. But just as quickly, the thought occurred to me, "what kid has never had a party?"

The reality, that kid would be me. This was my first party honoring me and it only took 25 years for me to be recognized. That took the breath out of me so, I probably did what I did best, which was to find something else to change me mood - something to deaden the feelings of sadness that seemed to always be lurking just below the surface waiting to engulf me. Feeling sad was an emotion I could definitely relate to but what made this different is that I finally was able to recognize how quickly even a joyous moment could be quickly overshadowed by sadness. The first time...

Path to healing:

Which parts of this chapter do you relate to?

What emotion/feelings(s) are you currently experiencing?

If you are ready to share your feelings, at this time, who would you share them with?

What do you need to do to create the opportunity to share?

Chapter 15
The First Time - I Fell in Love

The first time I fell in love, it completely took me by surprise. I had made up my mind a long time ago that I would be in control of my relationships and that I would call the shots. I would not be vulnerable and definitely would not leave myself open to being hurt, betrayed or abandoned. I had had enough of that during my childhood and was determined that I would never willingly put myself into any more situations that could possibly result in my experiencing those feelings again. With this goal in mind, I did not date. I did not do the "we go together thing." I did not want a boyfriend and if a guy was headed down that path, I quickly ended my interactions and moved on. For the most part, this worked for me.
What didn't work was that try as I might to avoid those soul crushing feelings, they still always lingered just below the surface - what I did not know was that the only solution to resolving this emotional turmoil is to actually deal with the feelings - to process them - to own them - to give myself permission to "feel what I was feeling," and grieve what I had lost. It was then and only then would I truly be able to move on and live life on life's terms.
But I digress, somewhat. My first marriage was to a guy who I met while I was highly intoxicated. I was so intoxicated that I had told my friend that I didn't think I should go to the party we had been planning to attend. We had been having a few drinks before heading out and I was rapidly headed to the stage where I could no longer gauge between being tipsy and flat out drunk ("one was too many and a thousand never enough.") But, she wanted to go to the party so I tagged

along. I don't remember actually ever entering the party because when we arrived I ran into my cousin who had invited us. He introduced me to his friend who offered me some drugs so instead of going into the party we got high in his car. This began what would eventually lead to a marriage that we were both too immature to manage but we tried.

A few months after our marriage, I became pregnant but experienced a miscarriage in the beginning of the second trimester. I was devastated - not because I necessarily "wanted a child" (I was ambivalent at best) and yet it seemed like the next logical step - "first comes love, then comes marriage, then comes _____ with a baby carriage." And yet the miscarriage jacked me up. I wondered if it was my fault because of my previous sexual history - I blamed myself. My concept of God, at that time was one who was vindictive and "kept score." I believed in a God who punished you for your misdeeds and I believed this because my aunt would frequently tell me when I did something wrong that I was going to "burst hell wide open." So I believed that the miscarriage was my fault and that we were being punished. I did not dare share my feelings of guilt and shame with my husband. What would he think about me? Would he blame me too?

He was equally as devastated by the miscarriage and tried, as best as he could to console me. For the next about 10 months, my goal was on getting pregnant again and each month when my period would come, I would sink deeper into a Depression. Finally, "the rabbit died" and it was confirmed that I was pregnant. Now I was happy and yet scared to death - just suppose it happened again. Just suppose it didn't and I messed around and carried the baby full term only to die giving birth? I have no idea where I had gotten that idea from but all I knew was that when I was a little girl I had heard someone say that giving birth was the closest a woman comes to death and I interpreted that as giving birth could kill you.

Again, I did not share any of my fears with my husband or anyone else. I just pretended that I was ok and figured if I pretended long enough, it just might be so. Eventually the day came when I proved my theory wrong and not only survived but gave birth to a 7lb 11oz baby boy. I know it almost sounds like a cliché' but something in me melted and for the first time, I fell in love dropping all of my defenses and the need to be in control of my feelings and keep myself safe.

The plan had been that I would return to work six weeks after the birth but by the end of week one, I knew I just couldn't do it. I could not leave my child with a stranger to care for him. How would they know what his various sounds meant? How would I trust someone else to take care of this little bundle of joy that had burst my heart wide open? I couldn't do it and went to my husband, crying and snotting as I tried to explain that I could not leave our child with any caregiver at all. My husband looked at me and said "so stay home." Initially I kept making my case of how I could not leave our son with anyone but eventually it finally sunk in just what he had said - "so stay home." To say I was shocked was an understatement.

Neither of us had what would be considered really good jobs and we really needed both salaries. And yet, he had given me my heart's desire - to be a full time stay at home mom. I was elated but I was also afraid because it slowly began to sink in that now, for the first time in my adult life, I would now become dependent on someone else to take care of me and emotionally, I was definitely not ready for that. And this was just the first time...

Path to healing:

Which parts of this chapter do you relate to?

What emotion/feelings(s) are you currently experiencing?

If you are ready to share your feelings at this time, who would you share them with?

What do you need to do to create the opportunity to share?

Chapter 16
The First Time - I "Really" Chose Sobriety

By the time I hit my thirties, my relationship with drugs and alcoholic had escalated exponentially. I was getting high on a regular basis and it was definitely impacting my daily functioning. Most evenings how I put myself and the children to bed was vague at best. I was smoking on the way to work and then leaving work during my lunch time to smoke some more.

While I fed the children their dinner, I would, more than likely, drink mine, so yes, most evenings ended in a blur. My then husband and I were marching hand and hand down this road to destruction and like any good "ghetto love" addicted couple, our daily pattern was to get high, argue, get high, argue some more…you get the picture.

I knew that this relationship was not healthy for any of us but when I would try to suggest that we separate, his response was that we were going to stay together until the boys were grown and then, and only then, maybe separate. While this response frustrated me, I made absolutely no moves to leave until one Saturday. We had been going through our regular routine (we had gotten high and were in the midst of an argument). My sister-in-law was over and was occupying the children. She later told me that my 2 year old son had said to her, "When people love each other they yell at each other." When she told me that, I felt appalled as well as ashamed and embarrassed. I made up my mind right then that something had to give. After she left, I packed a few bags for myself and the boys and went to a friend's house. Somehow or the other, my husband had become suspicious and eventually tracked me down at my friend's house.

This was before the days of cell phones and let me tell you - when I heard him banging on the door of my friend's place, I quickly fled (with the boys) to the bedroom. She would not allow him into the apartment and eventually he left. Two days later, the boys and I boarded a plane for DC. I had left my husband because I knew that our interactions were not healthy for any of us. I believed that if I had stayed that I would ultimately end up drinking myself to death and a small part of me wanted something better.

Now I say a small part because a part of me had actually given up caring and had resigned myself that "this was all that life had to offer." But, hearing those words from my son motivated me to take action - I removed us from our home but I didn't realize that I was taking myself and my addictions with me. I didn't fully grasp that the yelling, and bounced checks were not the only dysfunction in our home. I thought that if we could just separate then things might get under control.

Separation did change some of our dynamics but I was still operating with an active addiction. I quickly found a job and was able to get an apartment as well as a "piece of car." I developed a friendship with one of my co-workers who would spend a great deal of time telling me about his drug history. It seems that heroin had been his drug of choice. I would sit in amazement while I listened to the various experiences he would tell me from his life of active addiction. One of the reasons why I was so amazed is because he looked like

"Opie" from the Andy Griffin Show all grown up - he did not look like any of the dope fiends I had grown up with at all.

Anyway, one Monday after the Fourth of July holiday, I told him about how I had tried to get high all weekend and nothing seemed to work - I even smoked some "Love Boat" but it didn't affect me in the least. He listened attentively and then said "I want you to come with me somewhere during lunch." I didn't ask any questions, but simply said yes and didn't really catch on to where we were going until we entered a church fellowship hall and it quickly dawned on me that he had taken me to a 12 step meeting.

This hit me like a ton of bricks. To my way of thinking, this really solidified for me that that I was out of control. Now trust and believe, he was not the first person to imply or straight out tell me that I needed help - shoot I use to tell myself that on a regular basis and swear out that "this time" would be the last time. But that only lasted until the next time I picked up. So yes, I knew I was abusing alcohol as well as I knew that there was only one drug that I would not knowingly ingest and that was heroin, but that had not been motivation enough to do anything about it. And yet, when he took me to that meeting I finally hit me just how far I had sunk because I reasoned if someone who was as strung out as him believes that I have a problem, then this was an opinion I could respect.

At the conclusion of that first meeting, I asked my colleague to "pick me out a Sponsor" because the people in the meeting had been talking about the benefit of a Sponsor. He pointed someone out and I quickly went over to her and asked her to be my Sponsor and she said yes! That was July 1986 and on that day I fully committed to becoming clean and sober, one day at a time, one moment at a time, one step at a time.

In retrospect, I realize that I probably should have gone to treatment but my kids were 1 and almost three, I had left their dad and the idea of going to treatment was something I simply could not figure out how that could work. Needless to say, my first few days were hell. My body was definitely not use to this way of life but I hung in there and vowed to return back to that 12 step meeting. When I approached my colleague about accompanying me, he told me that he had relapsed (started using again) and then showed me a joint and asked if I wanted to get high with him. I was absolutely flabbergasted! It was almost as if I could not clearly decipher what he had very clearly stated, so as I stood there with my mouth hanging open, he repeated what he had just said - that he had relapsed and why don't I come and share that joint with him. As his words began to sink in, the biggest emotion I felt was fear. I was afraid to speak, afraid to get high, and afraid not to get high.

The blessing is that even as my conscious mind was totally perplexed and was in turmoil in what I should do, something deep within reminded me that I was done with that lifestyle. And yet even in my fear I was filled with gratitude that God had allowed my colleague to remain sober long enough to get me to a 12 step meeting before he himself relapsed. I'm not going to lie. A part of me was pissed that he was even offering the joint to me and I was also pissed that he had relapsed because I knew how far he had come but for once I put the focus completely on myself and I choose life and took my hind parts to that meeting without him. The first time...

Path to healing:

Which parts of this chapter do you relate to?

What emotion/feelings(s) are you currently experiencing?

If you are ready to share your feelings at this time, who would you share them with?

What do you need to do to create the opportunity to share?

Chapter 17
The First Time - Accepting Jesus for Myself

I have been baptized twice, once when I was about 10 and once at age 16. Neither time can I honestly say that I did it because (as all good church people know and can recite) I had accepted Christ as my personal Savior. I'm not really sure why I got baptized the first time – maybe it was peer pressure, maybe it was pressure from my Sabbath School Teacher, maybe…who knows? The second time it was definitely because my grandfather had told me and two of my cousins that it was time to get baptized, so I did but yet again, without any personal confession of faith. It would not be until I was in around 30 that I would have the experience of accepting Christ as my personal Savior in what might be considered an unorthodox situation - but more about that later.

My aunt was a Seventh Day Adventist and so every Saturday, we attended Ephesus Seventh Day Adventist Church. Exodus 20: 8-10 states:

8 Remember the Sabbath day, to keep it holy. 9 Six days shalt thou labour, and do all thy work: 10 But the seventh day is the Sabbath of the LORD thy God: in it thou shalt not do any work, thou; nor thy son; nor thy daughter; thy manservant; nor thy maidservant; nor thy cattle; nor thy stranger that is within thy gates.

Seventh Day Adventists believe that the Saturday begins at sundown Friday and continues until sundown Saturday. In our home, the Sabbath began with family devotion including song, reading and recitation of scripture and prayer. On

Saturday morning, we engaged in corporate worship beginning with Sabbath School followed by service. Communion was observed once per month and was preceded by foot washing. As described in an earlier chapter, being an Adventist for a child was kind of difficult. Back then, Adventist had a plethora of rules and dictates: no jewelry, no makeup, and no television or radio on the Sabbath. There were also dietary guidelines including no eating of any animal that the Bible had deemed as unclean which included pork, shellfish and any animal that were not cloven hoofed. And yet while all of the rules felt very confining, sitting in service was even more challenging for me.

From my perspective, the preacher seemed to only preach from the Old Testament and the book of Revelations. The messages tended to center around how awful we were as sinners and how, if we did not get our acts together, what would await us would be the fire and brimstone of hell. I don't remember hearing anything about grace, mercy, or love. The primary message seemed to always be centered on us being wretched sinners who had to earn the love of God.

They would reference, every now and then, about Jesus dying on a cross for our sins so that we could have everlasting life, but it seemed to always be followed by the idea that the only way we could possibly be a candidate for "everlasting life" would be if we worked really hard so that we could be deemed blameless before the throne and if all of this lined up maybe we might be considered worthy to enter heaven and walk those "streets paved with gold." I am sure my interpretation was very much influenced by my youth and

I am sure that the church folk were well meaning, but what I walked away with was what I now know was a much skewed belief system.

My interpretation of God was kind of like a score keeper. When I sinned, I got points in the bad column and when I did good points would go on the good side. The problem was it felt like I was racking up many, many more bad points so that eventually I just stopped trying. It felt like it was impossible to please God, so I resigned myself that this was yet one more thing that I had failed at.

My second baptism was in a Baptist church who, while they didn't have the same list of forbidden items of the Seventh Day Adventist Church, (church was now on Sunday, we could eat pork, wear jewelry and makeup and watch TV on Sunday), Capital View Baptist Church still had its own list of mandates. I had moved to DC to live with my mother and grandfather and my grandfather was very committed to church.

He was a Deacon and taught the adult Sunday school Class and if you lived in his house, come Sunday morning you got up and went to both Sunday school and church (well at least I did, my mother did not.) I attended and eventually taught Sunday school. I participated in Vacation Bible School and BTU (Baptist Training Union). If there was a program after church, we not only attended but in most instances we were active participants reciting scriptures and lines in the Christmas and Easter play. And yet, I still had not experienced a personal relationship with Jesus - I was simply following the program and doing what was expected. I mean, I can remember hanging out with my friends until the wee hours of the morning, taking a bath and heading up to the church to teach my Sunday school class - again, simply doing what was expected and not wanting to create any waves.

When I went away to college, this pattern continued. I connected with the Gospel service on campus and faithfully attended but still no personal connection. After college, my church attention became more and more sporadic until at the height of my addiction, I stopped attending all together. I suspect that on a subconscious level, I believed that I had accumulated too many "bad" points" - too many to ever earn enough good points to even balance them out, so I had quietly resigned myself to an ultimate fate of hell and damnation and, no I wasn't happy about it, but I felt too defeated to do anything about it.

It wasn't until I was around 30 and had begun to attend 12 step programs that I became exposed to another version/theology of God which was identified as Higher Power. The first three steps state:

1. We admitted we were powerless over alcohol—that our lives had become unmanageable.
2. Came to believe that a Power greater than ourselves could restore us to sanity.
3. Made a decision to turn our will and our lives over to the care of God as we understood Him.

The short version is:

Step1 - I can't
Step 2 - He can
Step 3 - Let him

Steps 4-12 referenced doing a moral inventory (self-evaluation) and then sharing that inventory with a trusted person.

Step 6 states:

"Were entirely ready to have God remove all these defects of character" followed by Step 7 which states: "Humbly asked Him to remove our shortcomings."

The next step is to make a list of everyone we have wronged followed by "making amends" (asking for forgiveness) to those we had wronged and to practice making amends as an ongoing way of life.

And while practicing Steps 1-10 were very important in helping me to maintain my sobriety, it was in practicing and witnessing the practice of Step 11 and 12 where I could finally say that I came to experience Jesus as my Personal Savior. Steps 11 and 12 state:

    11. Sought through prayer and meditation to improve our conscious contact with God as we understood Him, praying only for knowledge of His will for us and the power to carry that out.

    12. Having had a spiritual awakening as the result of these steps, we tried to carry this message to alcoholics, and to practice these principles in all our affairs.

Now you might say, nowhere in the Steps is Jesus specifically named. Nowhere in the Steps does it specifically focus on being pleasing to God, what you can and cannot do, say, eat or wear. And that, I believe is why I was able to finally have a personal relationship with God and accept Jesus into my heart and not just into my head. In these meetings, I got to witness "Jesus with skin," people who demonstrated the love of God in both word and deed.

People who were not judgmental and by their presence, offered a listening ear and did not tell me what to do (and not do) but simply shared their "experience, strength and hope" as a living demonstration of the love of God. The other thing that got my attention was that they didn't just welcome and embrace you if you stayed sober, no, even if you relapsed, even if you slipped and fell, their arms were still open in acceptance and the ongoing message was "keep coming back, it works if you work it." Even if you slipped up or even intentionally relapsed 1, 5, 20, 30+ times, if you could manage to stay clean 24 hours and came forward, you were given a 1 day chip with just as big of a smile as if you had never relapsed (or in church language, backslid).

Through those welcoming rooms, I learned to not be so hard on myself and to recognize that I was and continue to be a work in progress. I experienced not being made to feel that something was wrong with because my story was not like someone else's story. In those rooms, persons were not judged and filled with condemnation but rather were gently guided into a better way of life.

The churches I had attended had talked about the love of God but sometimes the doctrines and members actions implied that "love" was conditional - follow the rules and you will be loved. But in those 12 step rooms I encountered a visible manifestation of the unconditional love of God as demonstrated by acceptance whether I followed the rules or not. And yes, it was because of those rooms that I returned to church but this time with a new hunger and thirst to know more about this Jesus who gave his life for me with all of my flaws and challenges and became real to me through the unconditional love I experienced in those rooms.

It's interesting that when I stood before my ordination council, they asked me an interesting question - "why does the church fail in helping people dealing with addictions?" After a little thought, I responded because churches tend to be judgmental with an emphasis on "being right." My experience of 12 step rooms was an atmosphere of openness and acceptance and that is an atmosphere where I believe people can experience the love of Christ. Unconditional love and acceptance can sometimes be difficult to experience, but I am so grateful that I was able to experience this for the first time...

Path to healing:

Which parts of this chapter do you relate to?

What emotion/feelings(s) are you currently experiencing?

If you are ready to share your feelings at this time, who would you share them with?

What do you need to do to create the opportunity to share?

Chapter 18
The First Time - Confronting the Perpetrator

For a large part of my single life, I had no real desire to date. I was not seeking a boyfriend, boo or a bae. As a survivor of sexual molestation I would not have been able to identify a healthy relationship if I tried. When someone is introduced to sexual behavior before they are cognitively able to process what it is and before they are cognitively able to give informed consent, trying to have a relationship is like trying to do Algebra before you actually know the basic concepts of math.

Growing up, I had not witnessed many, if any healthy relationships at all. There weren't any couples that I could point to and say "I want what they have." Truth be told, I didn't even know what to want in a healthy relationship. All I really knew was that when you "fooled around" with a boy, it felt good and that was what got my attention. Having been molested for years, beginning at age 9, I didn't even know that what was cousin was doing to me had a name for it.

All I knew was that periodically I would find myself secluded somewhere with him and he would begin to do things to me that I didn't understand and at the conclusion I would be flooded with a sensation that felt good and yet I would also be filled with shame and guilt because even though I didn't know what to call what he was doing to me, I knew instinctively that it was wrong and deep down, I believed that it was my fault.

As I began to grow and my breasts began to sprout and my cousin found a new distraction (heroin), I began to attract the attention of the neighbor boys. Soon, I was all caught up in heavy petting and generating more of the "good" feelings that I both hated but also craved. As I came to the age where I could officially date, while my friends all wanted a boyfriend, as I stated earlier, I did not. All I wanted was the physical release but not the emotional commitment.

Now, my behaviors were not just about me "feeling good," and getting a physical release. It was also about me feeling in control. Truth be told, I never saw myself as being easy or being taken advantage of by my male partners. No, I saw myself as getting what I wanted on my own terms. In my mind, I was calling the shots and no longer felt like a victim. As I shared in a previous chapter, I kept this attitude through college, young single life and a first, substance riddled marriage. In this marriage I was committed, but mine and his addiction(s) made maintaining this relationship quite difficult. Fast forward to me separated with two sons. Each time I would meet someone and things looked like they were getting serious, I would back away using the excuse "I'm still married."

One day I was at a conference and the keynote speaker was a female therapist who was talking about the benefits of therapy. At the conclusion of her talk, I asked for her card with the intention of giving her a call for an appointment. It only took approximately three years for me finally call her practice and commit to therapy. I wasn't sure exactly what was wrong but by then, I knew that how I viewed relationships was a bit skewed.

My therapist helped me to see that there were some real deficits in how I viewed and mismanaged relationships particularly my propensity to "run" when the guy I was dealing with "began to catch feelings."

Eventually, I began to explore the molestation and this resulted in my writing a letter confronting my cousin, my perpetrator. After I had completed the letter and my therapist and I had processed it, I was then given the option to either destroy the letter, do nothing with the letter or to send it to my perpetrator. At the time he was in prison serving one of his many sentences. I made the decision to send the letter. I was not looking for a response. As a matter of fact, I did not want a response.

I had finally given myself permission to be angry with him and had worked hard on reducing my feelings of shame and guilt. All I wanted was to be able to tell him that his actions towards me had been wrong and how they had negatively impacted and continued to impact my life. I wasn't looking for an apology - I just wanted, and needed to be heard. So I mailed the letter.

Not long afterward, I received a letter from him which I was in no way, shape form or fashion ready to deal with. Just looking at the envelope reignited waves of anger and sadness deep inside of me and I was not ready to deal with anything he might have to say. A part of me was afraid that he would deny his actions, a part of me was afraid that he would try to minimize them or say that it was consensual and a part of me was afraid that he would apologize because if he did apologize, what would I do with my anger? So, with all of these conflicting feelings, I put the unopened letter aside and did not touch it for about 9 months.

Not long afterward, I received a call from my aunt (his mother) and my mother. My aunt reported that he had shared my letter with her and she had, in turn, shared it with my mother. My aunt's first question was "why didn't you tell me?" To which I responded "I didn't think you would believe me." I mean he was her son and, in my mind, I was "just" her niece. She reassured me that this was not the case and re-emphasized that she wished she had known. My mother, on the other hand, stated "The same thing happened to me when I was a child but it was by a woman. You learn to get over it."

Even in my shock, and yes, I was shocked that he had shared the letter with them, and I was shocked by my aunt's response because never in my wildest imagination had I ever thought that she would take my word over her son's. But the thing that shocked me the most was my mother's declaration that she too had been a victim of sexual abuse and her only advice was to "get over it."

Now the intellectual side of me understood that the "just get over" option was, for years the only option available to girls and women who were being raised in a society where they have been habitually undervalued. And yet, even with her years of demonstrated lack of parenting skills, something inside of me craved a response a little more "motherly", a little more empathetic, a little more caring. What I realize now is that she gave the best that she could offer given her experience and her context.

So, in retrospect, this chapter is not only about the "First time - confronting my perpetrator but also the first time confronting that sexual abuse was actually a generational curse. The first time...

Path to healing:

Which parts of this chapter do you relate to?

What emotion/feelings(s) are you currently experiencing?

If you are ready to share your feelings at this time, who would you share them with?

What do you need to do to create the opportunity to share?

Chapter 19
The First Time - I Tried to Reinvent Myself

As I look back over my life, an interesting thing occurred to me – that up until my mid-30's, I had never really dated. I know this might sound a bit crazy but let me first explain how I define dating. Dating, in my opinion, is when two people spend time in each other's company doing things together like going out for a meal, a movie, a show, a walk in the park - you get the idea - spending time together, in public.

As I have stated in an earlier chapter, as a result of my history of molestation, I had no real desire to date. My goal was to simply get what I wanted, enjoy intimate contact and avoid any emotional entanglements what so ever. That was my focus. That was how I ordered my life, and, for the most part, it worked quite well for me for a very long time until it didn't. At that point in my life, I had been married, two sons, divorced and my primary focus was on raising my children. But…I was still a woman with a healthy sexual appetite so I continued the behaviors that had served me well in the past - meet a man, have some fun and then bounce if I thought he was "catching feelings."

The challenge came when I inadvertently changed the formula - I met the man, but before we "had some fun" I found myself actually developing a friendship with him. Make no mistake, neither one of us were operating from a place of emotional wellness. We both had our own fair share of baggage. Neither of us had ever really experienced or really wanted a healthy relationship and yet we developed an incredible, sexually charged but not yet consummated relationship based on one of the most basic ingredients that a healthy relationship needs - we accepted each other with no judgments whatsoever. We shared about everything - the good, the bad and the ugly. We shared about the current people in our lives. We shared our hopes, our dreams and our fears. As time went by (about two years) we found that as much as we had connected, we both were able to verbalize that adding sex to our friendship had the potential to totally change our dynamic and neither one of us wanted to risk that.

But eventually, we took the plunge and to at least my surprise, I didn't have the desire to run when I realized that not only was he becoming more emotionally committed, but so was I. And yet, there was one major hurdle that challenged us. He was not able to maintain sobriety. We had met in a 12 step meeting and while I was amassing years of clean time, he would inevitably relapse time and time again. I eventually had to make, what I would come to feel was one of the toughest decisions of my life, which was to walk away from "us" because the reality is that it was becoming unhealthy for me. If making this decision was difficult, I can't begin to tell you how difficult it was to stick to my guns - but I did and he helped by respecting my decision. Yes, in a sense I was running again - but this time it hurt.

Fast forward to about a year later, therapy and a new man. Prior to meeting this man, I had spent almost a year of being celibate (something I had never done before) and was actually content with it after about the first few months. By happenstance I met a guy who displayed some qualities that had previously never been very important to me - he was working on a Master's Degree, he was conservative in his appearance, his temperament appeared to be relatively calm and he was not addicted to either drugs or alcohol. Somehow or the other, I made the decision that this must be the type of man and the type of lifestyle that I needed because wasn't that what "sober" people did? Like a number of women I have met, I had a thing for "bad boys" so the guys I tended to be attracted to tended not to be very conservative, had some familiarity with playing hard and fast and skirting along the boundaries of legal and illegal behaviors. To my way of thinking, I needed something totally different and this guy appeared to be just that. Now, granted I had no clear idea how to be conservative or some of the other traits that I found intriguing about him, but I decided to give it my best shot.

Prior to meeting him, I had been very involved with 12 Step programs and was Sponsoring a number of people. I frequently led meetings, chaired a meeting and attended the conventions and other activities. As I was getting to know this new guy, I told him my substance abuse history and while he said that he understood and added that substances had never really been an issue for him, if I introduced him to someone I knew from a 12 step meeting, he became a bit standoffish as a matter of fact, not necessarily flat out rude but definitely dismissive.

I quickly surmised that somehow or the other they were not acceptable to him so, because I had decided that who I was wasn't enough - because I had decided that my life needed a facelift, because I decided to reinvent myself, I slowly stopped going to meetings and slowly stop associating with the very people and program that had saved my life. Needless to say, it took me a lot of years, heartache, self-loathing, anger and just plain acting out behavior to realize that trying to reinvent myself was not the answer. As I worked hard at re-inventing myself, I began to realize that the person that I believed that my partner wanted me to be was not necessarily a person who I actually liked. Trying to be something or someone that I wasn't only left me depressed and very angry and I don't even like me when I am angry.

It took years for me to realize that self-acceptance is the key to walking in one's purpose and trying to reinvent myself into something I was not was definitely not the answer. I eventually "got" and began to learn to accept me with all of my flaws, blemishes, accomplishments and positive attributes. This was important because for the longest I had no idea what to say or do if someone complimented me - I had worked so hard for people not to really know me that if you complimented me I was convinced that you had no idea what you were talking about. But practicing intentional self-care and making peace with my past has taken me to a place where I no longer feel the need to reinvent myself because I am just fine being me. But this would not have been possible if there had not been a first time...

Path to healing:

Which parts of this chapter do you relate to?

What emotion/feelings(s) are you currently experiencing?

If you are ready to share your feelings, at this time, who would you share them with?

What do you need to do to create the opportunity to share?

"Be gentle. You are meeting parts of yourself you have been at war with."
Bad Ass Vegan (John Lewis)

Chapter 20
The First Time - Road to Forgiveness

The path of healing can be painful, takes courage and typically is begun with much fear and trepidation. Fear of hearing yourself speaking your horrible truth out loud - the truth that someone had violated you, used your body without your permission and as a result filled you with a lifetime of shame and guilt. Fear that you might not be believed and fear that someone would take your secret as truth. Fear that people would look at you differently, stigmatize you and even worse blame you for what had happened. We all know how that goes - "she shouldn't have worn that dress, she should have been more careful, and she must have led him on. And while there is never a justifiable reason why anyone should be forced to engage in a sex act, why anyone should be violated without their permission, why even if you are butt naked and say "No" why you "no" should be ignored with the faulty reasoning "you know you want it." No, there is never a justifiable reason to sexually assault anyone and when it comes to assaulting a child under the age of consent, the assault is even more egregious because a child's mind is still developing and is not fully formed until their early 20s. Children are innocent by nature and it is only the corruption and dysfunction of the adults in their world that destroys that innocence simply by an inappropriate touch, feel, lecherous look, etc. Once that happens, the world is no longer a safe place and that innocence that once was present, that allowed the child to see the world in wonder and amazement, is now replaced with increased anxiety, depression and feelings of guilt and shame. The child's response to this is to simply try to figure out how to survive in this new, unsafe, suspect environment. So, as a result of the assault, the child begins to develop coping skills to try to stay safe. They might overeat in the belief that if they become fat they will no longer be attractive. They might stop eating for the same reason. They might become withdrawn trying to sink inside of themselves so that they can't be noticed or they might act out in a desperate attempt to get the attention of the adults in their life so that maybe, just maybe someone will notice that something is wrong and rescue them.

The one thing they typically do not do is to tell anyone about what had happened to them and for the few that do take the risk to tell, many were told that either they were lying "the pastor/your dad, uncle, neighbor, cousin wouldn't do that." Or worse some are told, "I saw you flirting with him walking around here like you are grown." And some don't tell because they are afraid that their family will take justice into their own hands and kill the perpetrator and the child does not want that for their family. In "I Know Why The Cage Bird Sings" Maya Angelou writes that after her sexual assault, when her family found out, her assailant was never heard from again. So yes, there are many reasons why the child stays quiet and keeps the secret to themselves.

I didn't tell because I didn't really know what to tell. When the molestation started I was around 9 and hadn't a clue about what my cousin had actually been doing to me. All I knew was that it was scary, it made me feel dirty and I was definitely afraid that if I told, I would not be believed and worse would be sent to live in yet another home. So I kept quiet. I suffered in silence and I became sexually promiscuous in my attempt to no longer feel like a victim but more like the one who was calling the shots.

While being molested, I was scared and the worst part was that after a while, each and every time my body would betray me by responding to the stimulation and that only further confused me. It confused me because there were always two conflicting emotions present - fear and pleasure. It confused me because my assailant was my cousin who I had been raised with like a brother. He was someone who I looked up to and had made me laugh, played with me and defended me in the neighborhood on so many occasions. Bottom line, I really couldn't understand why he, of all people was doing that to me one minute and then in the next breath, behaving as if nothing had happened.

This is another reason why the sexual assault of a child is so problematic; because cognitively they really don't have the cognitive growth to even begin to process what they have experienced. This is why early intervention is so necessary but unfortunately, for a number of children and intervention of any kind doesn't come until much later if ever and, in a number of cases, after they have begun to act out in response to this violation of their innocence.

My journey in therapy didn't begin until I was in my early 30s and then it was long and arduous. It began with me trying to figure out why I was so quick to abandon relationships simply because the guy was "getting closer" and wanting more than sex. It would take me some time to finally reveal the sexual molestation, and even longer to correlate my behaviors as responses to what I had experienced. The course of treating sexual assault typically follows the trajectory of the patient breaking the silence and giving voice to the unspeakable - telling what happened. That is challenging in itself because as the story is shared, the feelings come right along with it and those feelings tend to be so intense that it is hard to distinguish between what is real and what is a memory. If the nightmares had not already been present, this is probably the point where they will either resurface or begin with a vengeance. As I forced myself to stay in the process and not run away from therapy by making excuses like "that therapist just doesn't get it, I don't like him/her," or simply "this is just too hard" I found myself becoming consumed with anger. I was angry at my cousin, angry at the adults in my life for not protecting me, and angry at all men. I was also angry towards everyone who had not been assaulted. They got to maintain their innocence and I had not.

My therapist encouraged me to get the anger out as well as the other emotions that were under the anger like sadness, sorry, loneliness and pain. Then there was the letter writing and confronting my cousin and after that, the last and finally step was exploring the land of forgiveness; forgiveness of self, forgiveness of the adults in my life who failed to protect me and forgiveness of my cousin.

This was not an easy task and it definitely did not happen overnight or even after a few sessions. This took a lot of processing, soul searching and finally the determination that I was tired of the weight of staying in the land of unforgiveness. Staying in that place did not allow me to grow. It did not allow me to learn to love myself, to honor myself and to finally stop defining myself by my body. And yet while I struggled with forgiving, while I vacillated between wanting to just rest in depression, and wanting to kill him, what I realized was that what I really wanted was peace, love and joy and none of those things could come into my life until I could honestly and fully forgive.

So, I eventually made the decision to forgive. I reminded myself of this decision when someone would call my cousin's name, or when we were in each other's company at family gatherings. I would remind myself of this when I found myself considering operating from that old familiar place of shame and guilt. And I would remind myself, when challenged to take agency over my body, remembering that I now had choices about my sexual encounters and more importantly that I was more than just a body with large breasts. I choose forgiveness because I have been in the place where I was the one who was seeking to be forgiven and how could I ask that of someone if I was unable to forgive someone else.

There was no "aha" moment. There wasn't flashing lights or an audible voice but rather it was an intentional decision to forgive. It was as simple as that and with that the bars that had held me down opened and allowed me to fully experience all that life has to offer.

If you have gotten to this point, my prayer is that if you too are victim of sexual assault, I pray that in sharing my journey, you will find parts of yourself - the hidden parts that you have tried so hard to ignore. My prayer is that you will begin to understand why you do some of the things you do and then begin the process of getting help that will put you fully on the path to ultimate healing.

If you have been blessed to never having experienced sexual assault, then I pray that this book has enlightened you and then propelled you to protect your children, listen to your children, pay attention to your children and if they say that they don't want to hug someone, don't make them. Become an advocate for the victims and don't re-victimize them with judgmental comments and a lack of compassion. And finally, love them - be a visible demonstration of the love of Christ with skin. The path to forgiveness begins with a first time.

Path to healing:

Which parts of this chapter do you relate to?

What emotion/feelings(s) are you currently experiencing?

If you are ready to share your feelings, at this time, who would you share them with?

What do you need to do to create the opportunity to share?

"You either get bitter or you get better. It's that simple. You either take what has been dealt to you and allow it to make you a better person or you allow it to tear you down. The choice does not belong to fate, it belongs to you." Josh Shipp

Summary
The First Time – Reclaiming Your Voice

My editor suggested to me that this book could benefit from a summary type of chapter that included Lessons that I learned as well as what I want the reader to take from this book. This was a bit of a challenge for me because, as noted previously, all of the behaviors and experiences that are described in the book happened more than once, so clearly it took me multiple times to finally reach a place of wholeness and acceptance. But the good news is that, slowly but surely, I began to heal. And if I can heal, so can you and while you might be thinking "she just doesn't know my story," you are right, I don't but what I do know is that you are fearfully and wonderfully made and healing is available if you are willing to pursue it.

As you begin your path to healing, first and foremost, understand what a wonderful gift you are giving yourself. No more living in shame, displacing your anger and mistrust on those who around you because you fear that if they only knew the "real" you that they would judge you and your actions. By embarking on the road to healing, you are proclaiming that you will no longer be held captive by those negative emotions and beliefs that have guided your life and interactions. Healing equals the freedom to live to your full potential, unapologetically loving yourself without reservation. So let's begin the process of healing:

It's not your fault - you are not responsible for what happened to you. You were a child who was taken advantage of - who was introduced to sexual behavior/materials before you were cognitively able to process it. The fault lies solely with the perpetrator who harmed you. Now repeat after me "It's not my fault."

You are not what happened to you - As I stated earlier, as a result of my abandonment and sexual abuse issues, I began early on to define myself as "unlovable, messed up, a victim." In addition, I began to believe that the only thing I had to offer was my body. While that was what my child "mind" had determined to be true, what I learned is that there is so much more to me. I am smart, I am kind, I can be an interesting conversationalist (when I want to) and what I have to say matters - I do have a voice. And guess what, so do you.

Boundaries are good - I was raised in households that had a lot of rules but, in retrospect, little boundaries. What I have come to learn is that boundaries are not only good but, more importantly, they are necessary. The first boundary that I learned to set was simply to say "no." Growing up, I never believed that I had a choice about anything so I learned to simply remain silent. The problem with that is that my silence was often interpreted as agreement, as acquiescence, as my saying yes, giving my approval. Discovering that I could say "no" was an act of Freedom and allowed me to begin the journey towards self-determination. Very closely related to learning to say "no," was discovering that everyone does not deserve or should even warrant my time and/or attention simply because that is what they want. Another boundary that I was finally able to put in place is that I don't have to stay where I am uncomfortable, I don't have to tolerate mistreatment or try to get someone to like/love me particularly if it means not allowing myself to live authentically. What I have learned is that I have the power to choose and that my choices are predicated on what is healthy for me from a holistic perspective and not simply because my hormones are "acting up," which leads me to the next statement:

Feelings aren't fact - This is something that took me some time to learn, but is essential to the healing process. Just because I feel something, not only doesn't make it true but also doesn't mean that I have to act on every feeling I experience. Feelings come and go. Some feelings are justified (based on the situation) and some, well let's be honest, are just "knee jerk" reactions to old wounds that have been reopened and have little to do with what is presently going on. For example, if my instinct is to "go off" on someone because I "feel" that they were trying to take advantage of me, I have learned to ask myself the following questions:

- What is the evidence to support this feeling that I am being taken advantage of?
- What is the evidence that does not support this feeling?

Asking myself these two questions are extremely important because due to my history of having been victimized, my first instinct is to not trust, and my ultimate goal is to keep myself safe. Before I began this process of self- discernment, I allowed my emotions to take over and all I knew was that the "scared, vulnerable little girl" needed to be safe, by any means necessary. So I would "go off." This process of healing has taught me that feelings are not always fact and old wounds can be reopened. The blessing is that I can now give myself the time to process first before I act which then opens the door to the realization that not everything needs to be acted upon immediately or in some instances, ever. In other words "in the grand scheme of things, how much does this believed slight actually matter?" And even if it does matter on some level, by challenging whether or not my feelings are "fact," allows me to determine how much energy I want to give this unprocessed feeling.

Be afraid but do it anyway - One of the responses to a trauma can be increased anxiety - a fear of what could be, of what could happen in the future. I lived my life captive to a plethora of fears. I was afraid to be seen, afraid to be heard, afraid to be rejected and afraid to be accepted. I was afraid to be cared about but equally afraid of being left to fend on my own. An acronym for fear is False Evidence Appearing Real. The reality is that we cannot predict the future with any real certainty. Yes there are some variables that might make a prediction a little more accurate, but ultimately we don't have the ability to accurately predict the future. Trauma clothes life from a position of fear and distrust and while yes there are people in the world who are operate from a position of distrust, and yes there are some things that we should have a healthy fear about, moving outside of our comfort zones and taking healthy risks are all a part of healthy growth. Once I began to allow myself to push forward in spite of my fears, my world and interactions with others began to change for the better. I began to realize that my fear of being found to be inadequate and not good enough was not just my fear, but the fear of so many others. I began to understand how fear had been preventing me from enjoying the beauty that this life has to offer because I had been so focused on the negative - the "what could go wrong" as oppose to "what could go right." The bottom line is that we have a choice to either allow fear to continue to paralyze us or to push past the fear and simply acknowledge "I'm afraid, but I am going to pursue the good things in life in spite of my fear."

Accept help - I suspect that early on I began to operate under the belief that I needed to be self- sufficient - that no one was going to help me. Because of my childhood, it was difficult to determine who was in my corner and who was not. Remember my perpetrator was a family member and for a significant portion of my life, my birth parents were MIA (missing in action). I was so afraid of rejection and/or being hurt, that I learned early on to figure stuff out on my own. The problem was that I was operating from a limited knowledge bank and some of my decisions were not the best (to say the least). Unfortunately, this radical self-reliance continued long into my adulthood until I slowly began to realize that my life was not going the way I wanted,

I didn't know why, and I was going to need help if I wanted to find this thing called joy and happiness. Now the challenge in "Seeking Help" is moving through the fear that says that people can't be trusted. Now make no mistake, there are some untrustworthy people out there, but there are also some folk out there who have your best interest at heart. I encourage you to take this leap of faith, and reach out and ask for help. There are licensed professional Therapists and Counselors who can support you through the process of reclaiming your voice. Take a risk and reach out because you not only deserve it but you are worth it.

The best is yet to come - My closing message to you dear reader is that "the best is yet to come." You have been through some things which have affected every significant area of your life but this is your time to reclaim you. This is your time to begin the process of healing, self- acceptance and self- love. This is your time to practice radical forgiveness beginning with forgiving yourself. This is the time to begin to live authentically and explore the gifts and talents that reside in you. You are fabulous. You are fearfully and wonderfully made and if you can't quite believe this right now, then simply remind yourself that I believe this about you. It's your time, it's your season. Make peace with your past and walk boldly into your future.

I would love to hear updates on how you are progressing on your journey of healing and restoration. I can be reached at Firstime.beginnings@gmail.com

Thank you for being you.

Made in the USA
Columbia, SC
18 March 2020